Cambridge Elements ≡

Elements in the Philosophy of Mind
edited by
Keith Frankish
The University of Sheffield

ATTENTION AND MENTAL CONTROL

Carolyn Dicey Jennings
University of California

Shaftesbury Road, Cambridge CB2 8EA, United Kingdom

One Liberty Plaza, 20th Floor, New York, NY 10006, USA

477 Williamstown Road, Port Melbourne, VIC 3207, Australia

314–321, 3rd Floor, Plot 3, Splendor Forum, Jasola District Centre,
New Delhi – 110025, India

103 Penang Road, #05–06/07, Visioncrest Commercial, Singapore 238467

Cambridge University Press is part of Cambridge University Press & Assessment,
a department of the University of Cambridge.

We share the University's mission to contribute to society through the pursuit of
education, learning and research at the highest international levels of excellence.

www.cambridge.org
Information on this title: www.cambridge.org/9781108987066
DOI: 10.1017/9781108982269

First published 2022

A catalogue record for this publication is available from the British Library.

ISBN 978-1-108-98706-6 Paperback
ISSN 2633-9080 (online)
ISSN 2633-9072 (print)

Attention and Mental Control

Elements in the Philosophy of Mind

DOI: 10.1017/9781108982269
First published online: November 2022

Carolyn Dicey Jennings
University of California

Author for correspondence: Carolyn Dicey Jennings, cjennings3@ucmerced.edu

Abstract: Mental control refers to the ability we have to control our own minds. Its primary expression, attention, has become a popular topic for philosophers in the past few decades, generating the need for a primer on the concept. It is related to self-control, which typically refers to the maintenance of a preferred behavior in the face of temptation. While mental control is a distinct concept, criticisms of self-control can also be applied to mental control, such as that it implies the existence of an unscientific homunculus-like agent or is not a natural kind. Yet, as this Element suggests, a scientifically grounded account of mental control remains possible. The Element is organized into five main sections, which cover the concept of mental control, the relationship between mental control and attention, the phenomena of meditation and mind wandering, attention deficit hyperactivity disorder, and emergence-based accounts of mental control, including an original account by the author.

This Element also has a video abstract: www.cambridge.org/
Jennings_abstract

Keywords: mind, attention, control, emergence, neuroscience

ISBNs: 9781108987066 (PB), 9781108982269 (OC)
ISSNs: 2633-9080 (online), 2633-9072 (print)

Contents

1 Prologue

Mental control refers to the ability we have to control our own minds. This may be accomplished by focusing our mental energy on a particular task, drumming up motivation for a particular action, inhibiting distractors or temptations, bringing various mental events into alignment, or perhaps even moving the body or moving to a specific environment in order to change our pattern of thinking. Take the example of playing ping-pong with friends: one uses mental control to focus on the location of the ball in space, to remain engaged at the end of a long rally, to ignore friends who are talking nearby, to coordinate one's conversation around the difficulty of play, and perhaps when moving one's body to a ready position, to better see and respond to a serve.

"Mental control" makes little showing in philosophy. Yet, the primary expression of mental control – attention – has become a more popular topic for philosophers in the past few decades. While scientists wrote extensively on attention in the twentieth century, philosophers focused on consciousness. In the twenty-first century, greater engagement between philosophy and the sciences led to more scientific exploration of consciousness and more philosophical analysis of attention. This Element thus focuses on mental control through the phenomenon of attention, while also covering some related topics (mind wandering and attention deficit hyperactivity disorder [ADHD]) and some general issues in the metaphysics of mind (mental causation and emergence). Because there is so little work on mental control as a broader concept, the Element is limited in providing a thorough analysis and review. It nonetheless provides some initial analysis of this concept, which should indicate a path for future work.

While philosophers have written little on the concept of mental control, they have written extensively on self-control. Mental control is broader than the concept of self-control, which typically refers to the maintenance of a preferred behavior in the face of temptation. Nonetheless, criticisms of the concept of self-control can also be applied to the concept of mental control. In particular, the criticism that self-control implies the existence of an unscientific *homunculus-like agent* also threatens mental control (see, e.g., Sripada 2021). Relatedly, the charge that self-control is *not a natural kind* can also be levied against mental control (see, e.g., Herdova 2017). Yet, this Element will leave open the possibility that a philosophically plausible and scientifically grounded account of mental control remains possible, at least when understood through the concept of attention.

This Element is organized as follows. First, it describes the phenomenon of mental control and nearby forms of control. Second, it covers the relationship between mental control and attention, including the debate on whether mental control can be automatic. Third, it discusses the phenomenon of both meditation and mind wandering and how they relate to attention and mental control. Fourth, it closely examines a disorder of mental control, ADHD. Finally, it addresses the issue of emergence, one framework for thinking about mental control, discussing both traditional and contemporary accounts of emergence and how they might support mental control. That section puts forward a how-possible account of emergent mental control that makes use of contemporary neuroscience.

A guiding principle of what follows is that mental control is a necessary part of our understanding of the mind, and that further philosophical and scientific work on the topic is thus crucial not only for a complete account of mental control but for a host of other philosophical debates that depend on our understanding of the mind (e.g. legal theory). The Element is thus as necessary as it is incomplete, yet I hope it will serve as a guide for those who would continue this important project.

2 What Is Mental Control?

As James might have said, everyone knows what mental control is. While this may be true in a general sense, a precise understanding is more elusive. The term was not widely used before Wegner's critical work on the subject, starting with the "white bear study" (Wegner et al. 1987).[1] As one psychologist puts it, "There is not any specialized history of conceptions of mental control as there is of memory, sensation, or various other cognitive processes" (Schneider 1993, 33). Wegner thus starts with an intuitive definition: "Normally, we seem to have a measure of control over our thinking" (Wegner 1988, 683). Use of the term remains closely tied to both the intuitive notion and Wegner's own work.[2] In this section I aim to draw out contemporary use of the concept while connecting it with nearby work in philosophy.

According to the intuitive use of the term introduced above, mental control is control *of* the mind *by* the mind: *We* seem to have a measure of control over *our thinking*. How this occurs is not well understood, so it is often illustrated

---

[1] Wegner and Pennebaker report in 1993 that "the term *mental control* does not appear in searches of the psychological literature prior to 1987" (3). With the benefit of the Internet I did note some earlier mentions, albeit few. One such mention from around the same time period is the finding of a link between mental control and depression, also explored in a later study (Strömgren 1977; Breslow, Kocsis, and Belkin 1980). As it is used in these other studies, mental control "is probably most clearly associated with aspects of memory functioning which concern attending to the task" (Breslow, Kocsis, and Belkin 1980, 542).

[2] Of the top ten articles yielded by a search in Google Scholar for "mental control" in May 2022, eight include Wegner as an author.

Table 1 Mental control is control of the mind by the mind and can be contrasted with nearby forms of control involving the mind and body

Control of:		Control by:	
		the mind	external factors
	the mind	mental control	mind control
	behavior	action control	sensorimotor control

through everyday examples: "Mental control occurs when people suppress a thought, concentrate on a sensation, inhibit an emotion, maintain a mood, stir up a desire, squelch a craving, or otherwise exert influence on their own mental states" (Wegner and Pennebaker 1993, 1). Recall the ping-pong example from Section 1: In order to play a better game, we might suppress distracting thoughts, concentrate on the ball in flight, inhibit a fear of failure, maintain a sense of calm, stir up the desire to win, or squelch a craving for tasty snacks nearby. All of these would count as forms of mental control.

Excluded is control of other functions by the mind, such as behavior.[3] While one might reasonably interpret the term this way, "the current renaissance in the area of mental control has largely been fueled by those who have taken the meaning in the narrow sense – that is, as an attempt to control thoughts and thought processes" (Schneider 1993, 13). Likewise excluded is control of the mind by external factors, such as other agents. Some explicitly contrast mental control with, for instance, "sensorimotor control": While mental control is "induced intentionally," sensorimotor control is "perceptually (externally) induced and is controlled by recent environmental stimuli" (Schack and Frank 2021, 530). Thus, while the words "mental" and "control" are broad, and one might be tempted to judge their combination to include any place where the two overlap, specialist use of the term is more restricted (see Table 1). Given the potential for confusion, "mental control" is sometimes used with modifying language, such as "personal-level mental control" (Papineau 2015), which can help to distinguish it from these other forms of control.

In their introduction to *The Handbook of Mental Control* (1993), Wegner and Pennebaker explicitly tie mental control to attention: "A view of attention as the central faculty of mental control is part of much contemporary work in cognitive

---

[3] This includes work on the concept of behavioral control, which is a separate topic that has received much more attention in philosophy (see, e.g., Shepherd 2014; Christensen, Sutton, and McIlwain 2016). This distinction is analogous to that between mental action and bodily action, which are sometimes treated as separate topics (see, e.g., Fiebich and Michael 2015).

psychology" (4).[4] Mirroring typical accounts of attention, they contrast mental control with automaticity, in which case the mind is "beyond our control" (4). While they see this divide as one that overlaps with thorny issues, such as the problem of free will, they take it to be tractable through an operational approach. They thus argue that mental control can be operationally separated from "unintended but appropriate mental activity" using a range of experimental techniques (8). These experimental techniques include, among others, (a) using parallel tasks to determine the use of cognitive resources thought to be limited in mental control; (b) observing somatic markers, such as behavioral freezing in the face of mental conflict, typically associated with an attempt at mental control; and (c) collecting self-reports from participants as to whether they are using mental control.

For the most part, scientists now study mental control through what they call "executive control." Broadly speaking, "executive" functions support the coordination and management of other mental functions; they include "inhibition . . . working memory, and cognitive flexibility" (Diamond 2013, 135). Executive *control* is taken to include a subset of the executive functions – those that direct other mental functions in the service of tasks or goals: "It is needed to overcome local considerations, plan and orchestrate complex sequences of behavior, and prioritize goals and subgoals" (Miller and Wallis 2009, 99). In some cases, executive control is treated as control by a "central executive," or a unitary system of control, explicitly making use of a homunculus-like figure (Baddeley 1996, 1998; see subsection 3.2 for discussion of the homunculus). The more popular contemporary perspective is to see executive control as distributed across several systems (see, e.g., Logie 2016). In both cases, "prefrontal cortex" is likely to play a crucial role, because prefrontal cortex is domain general, and thus an ideal candidate for controlling domain-specific neural networks (Stuss and Alexander 2000; Figure 1e–i). As Buehler (2018) puts it, "Central executive control is likely implemented through the prefrontal cortex's modulation of neural activity in domain specific neural networks" (1974).

Buehler (2018) identifies three core functions of executive control: switching, maintenance, and inhibition. Prominent behavioral tests used to explore these functions include the Wisconsin Card Sorting Test (WCST) and Stroop Task (see, e.g., Derrfuss et al. 2005). The WCST involves the participant choosing one out of four possible cards to match a card that is provided. While the participant is not provided with the underlying rule to help them

---

[4] Schneider, for instance, divides mental control into three types, with attention supporting the most central type: "We control our thoughts by manipulating our sense organs (external control), by voluntary focus of attention (direct control), and by initiating trains of thought (indirect control)" (1993, 28).

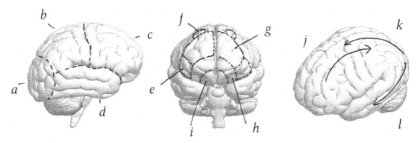

Figure 1 Views of the brain and select brain areas. On the far left is a view of the brain from the right, including (a) occipital or visual cortex, (b) parietal cortex, (c) frontal cortex (including prefrontal areas), and (d) temporal cortex. In the middle is a view of the brain from the front, including (e) ventral lateral prefrontal cortex (right hemisphere is indicated, but each area occurs in both hemispheres), (f) frontal eye fields (FEF), (g) dorsolateral prefrontal cortex (dlPFC), (h) orbitofrontal cortex, and (i) ventral medial prefrontal cortex (vmPFC). On the far right is a view of the brain from the top left, including (j) frontoparietal feedback, (k) dorsal visual pathway (feedforward), and (l) ventral visual pathway (feedforward).

determine the correct card, there are three possible rules: matching the color of the objects on the cards, matching the shape of those objects, and matching the number of objects. The participants can determine the rule through feedback, but the rule may change over a session. The WCST measures how well the participant identifies, maintains, and switches between these rules. The Stroop Task, on the other hand, requires the participant to report on one of the features of a stimulus while ignoring a more salient feature. Typically, a participant will be asked to report on the color of a word while the word itself is a conflicting color term (e.g. the word "blue" in red ink would require the participant to say "red"). The Stroop Task thus measures how well the participant is able to inhibit the salient feature in service of the task at hand. These and other behavioral tests have allowed scientists to determine the scope and limits of executive control, as well as its neurobiological basis.

While there have been some successes in the experimental domain, philosophical work is needed: "Mental control has proven to be an elusive target for scientific analysis, embedded as it is in sticky philosophical problems such as volition and dualism" (Vallacher 1993, 444). Philosophers have, unfortunately, published little on mental control.[5] As is mentioned in Section 1, mental control

---

[5] The same is true for executive control. As Buehler puts it: "Surprisingly, philosophers have not much engaged with the scientific literature on executive functioning" (2018, 1969). "Executive

includes within it the more popular topic of self-control, which appears in sixty-eight separate entries of *The Stanford Encyclopedia of Philosophy* (*SEP*). The term "mental control" shows up only once, in a single entry https://plato.stanford.edu/archives/sum2020/entries/testimony-episprob/. It is thus natural to start a philosophical discussion of mental control with a brief discussion of self-control.

While self-control is often described in terms of overcoming temptation, a broad definition might note the "competition between smaller sooner (SS) rewards and larger later (LL) rewards . . . [such that] the presence of SS rewards places the agent in a situation of conflict and requires the exercise of self-control" (Kennett and Wolfendale 2019, 34). A classic example is that of the marshmallow task: children are asked which of two options they prefer, one or two marshmallows, and then told that if (and only if) they wait they can have their preferred option. That is, the child can only have the preferred two marshmallows if they are able to refrain from eating the single marshmallow placed in front of them (Shoda, Mischel, and Peake 1990). Famously, the longer a child is able to wait, the more academic success they exhibit in adolescence: "Coherent patterns of statistically significant correlations were found between seconds of delay time in such conditions in preschool and cognitive and academic competence and ability to cope with frustration and stress in adolescence" (Shoda, Mischel, and Peake 1990, 978). These findings were later replicated and extended, leading to the insight that self-control is a "critical early capacity" (Watts, Duncan, and Quan 2018).[6]

Kennett and Wolfendale go beyond the above definition to provide a taxonomy of self-control, noting the different *methods* and *levels* of self-control (2019). In terms of methods, they separate "exerting willpower" from "implementing strategies" as well as "synchronic" from "diachronic" self-control. Take the example of waiting for two marshmallows: one might exert willpower to help one wait or one might implement a strategy, such as looking away from the single marshmallow. Willpower is necessary to overcome a temptation at the time it is given (synchronic) in lieu of a strategy, but strategies can be used if planned in advance of the temptation or for ongoing temptations (diachronic). As willpower is limited, the bulk of self-control depends on strategies enacted diachronically (see, e.g., Bermúdez 2021).

---

control" shows up in three entries of the *SEP*: "David Hartley," "Neuroethics," and "Philosophical Psychopathology," each time as a single mention.

[6] Worth noting are the structural and social features found to predict success on the marshmallow task, including caregiver reliability, which may or may not predict success through an impact on mental control (Duckworth, Tsukayama, and Kirby 2013; Kidd, Palmeri, and Aslin 2013; Lamm et al. 2018; Michaelson and Munakata 2020). Moreover, the task has not been found to predict other, later outcomes, such as "mid-life capital" (Benjamin et al. 2020).

In terms of levels, Kennett and Wolfendale separate "intentional," "instrumental," and "normative" self-control, with intentional serving as the lowest level. Intentional control requires only the involvement of an intention, instrumental control requires the ability to achieve that intention through intermediate steps, and normative control requires that the entire process is sensitive to considered judgments and values. Kennett and Wolfendale argue that to be an agent at all one would need intentional control, to be an agent over time one would need instrumental control, and to flourish as an agent one would need normative control. They find the importance of self-control to be best displayed in this highest level: "Self-control is a necessary condition of access to a variety of goods that help constitute a life as meaningful, as flourishing, and, importantly, as one's own" (Kennett and Wolfendale 2019, 38).

One might construe self-control through the language of "first-order" and "higher-order" desires (see, e.g., Frankfurt 1988). As Holton and Shute put it: "Accounts agree that self-control consists in a particular kind of control over one's actions – in each case the obvious contrast is with actions that are driven purely by one's (first-order) desires" (2007, 51). Higher-order desires are desires *about* first-order desires. Desiring the marshmallow, for instance, is a first-order desire, while wanting to squelch the desire for the marshmallow is a second-order desire. In self-control, our first-order desires are in conflict with higher-order desires, and we aim to resolve that conflict in favor of the higher-order desires. We might see this as *self-shaping*, since the process ultimately alters the relative strength of our desires. Kane (1999) describes, for example, a case in which a businesswoman decides to stop and help a victim of assault rather than continue on to an important meeting. She has competing desires – to help the victim and to continue on to her meeting – and resolves them in favor of the former.[7] This is a case, Kane argues, in which the businesswoman's effective desire (her "will") was not already determined, but she helped determine it through her action, making it more likely in the future that she would stop to help a victim in the face of a conflicting desire (Kane 1999, 224).

How do these considerations intersect with mental control? While there is significant overlap between self-control and mental control, there is also difference. Take the list provided by Wegner, above: "suppress a thought," "inhibit an emotion," and "squelch a craving" are all strongly associated with self-control. Yet, the other items on the list are less clearly associated. When we "concentrate

---

[7] While it may not be obvious from the description here, I am treating the desire to continue on to the meeting as a first-order desire, and the desire to stop to help the victim as a higher-order desire (a desire to overcome this first-order desire). This fits Kane's narrative of the businesswoman overcoming temptation in favor of her "moral conscience" (Kane 1999, 225).

Table 2 Points of contrast between self-control and mental control

	Self-control	Mental Control
Source	higher-order desires	the mind
Target	first-order desires	any mental state or function
Method	willpower or strategy	switching, maintenance, or inhibition
Outcome	self-shaping (change to the desire system)	mind shaping (change to any mental disposition)

on a sensation" are we necessarily overcoming temptation? How about when we "maintain a mood" or "stir up a desire"? The language of "temptation" comes from the close ties between philosophical research on self-control and discussions of normativity; mental control is disconnected from those considerations. Further, while self-control concerns the conflict between smaller sooner and larger later rewards, mental control may also include conflict within these levels (between different types of smaller sooner rewards or different types of larger later rewards). Finally, mental control can result in long-term changes, but these need not be to our desires. If I concentrate on the ping-pong ball, I am not necessarily shaping my desires but rather my perceptual and motor capacities. Thus, mental control can be seen as a broader umbrella under which self-control falls, with self-control specifically describing cases of conflict resolution between higher-order and first-order desires, or larger later and smaller sooner rewards, that results in some degree of self-shaping or a change to the desire system (see Table 2).[8]

As mentioned earlier, attention is often cited as the key to mental control. Recall that mental control is studied scientifically through executive control, sometimes understood as control by a central executive. In fact, the "central executive" initially proposed by Baddeley and Hitch (1974) was just attention, as can still be seen in most descriptions of the model (see, e.g., Parkin 1998, 518). While Baddeley has since argued that we should break up the central executive into subcomponents, "including dual task performance, attentional focusing, attention switching, and interfacing with [long-term memory],"

---

[8] I take these considerations to be separable from temporal ones. Sripada (2021), for example, has argued that self-control occurs over an extended period and is built up from short duration cognitive control states. The account above covers both short-duration mental control (e.g. a single instance of Stroop inhibition) as well as long-duration mental control (e.g. task maintenance and switching in WCST).

attention still plays the primary role (1998, 525). As described by Buehler, "Sometimes this aspect of executive functioning is called 'executive attention'" (2018, 1970). In the next section I will review work that ties mental control to attention, as well as work that challenges this perspective on mental control.

3 Attention and Mental Control

As we saw in the previous section, attention comes up frequently in discussions on mental control. What is attention? Like mental control, its meaning is at once familiar and elusive, with many competing accounts of the phenomenon within philosophy.[9] Consider the example of attending to a dinner guest: we might "pay attention" to the guest one moment, while our attention is "grabbed" by the doorbell the next. That attention can be "paid" and "grabbed" indicates that it has something to do with mental resources, and, in fact, a commonly cited feature of attention is that it is resource limited.[10] Attention is typically described as the process of *prioritizing* these resources.[11] One might say that attention is the prioritization of some mental processes over others, often resulting in the selection of one or more mental processes at the expense of others.

Importantly, attention is not the only selective process in the brain. The selection of particular light wavelengths in the eye is not attention, for example (see, e.g., Mariani 1984). The prioritizing work of attention is best seen as occurring in concert with other forms of prioritization and selection, such as the prioritization of naturally salient stimuli. That is, stimuli that are strong smelling, bright, fast moving, or loud "grab" one's attention due to processes other than attention that prioritize those stimuli (see, e.g., Reynolds and Desimone 2003). Attention theorists are divided on how exactly to separate attention from these other selective processes, but most philosophers describe attention as a "personal" or "subject-level" phenomenon – a phenomenon that essentially involves the person or subject, rather than a proper part of the person or subject – with substantial variance on how to interpret these terms. For example, while Wu (2011) holds that "the subject level process notion should be understood as *selection for action*" (97), Jennings (2012) holds that attention

---

[9] These range from Mole's (2011) "adverbial" view – that attention is not a process but a way that mental processes might proceed – to Prinz's (2011) "AIR" view that "attention is a process by which perceptual representations become available to working memory" (186).

[10] One potential neural resource is glucose, a general resource for demanding cognitive tasks (Ampel, Muraven, and McNay 2018).

[11] Take, for instance, Buehler's (2019) definition: "Attending to something, in its broadest, most widely accepted sense, involves the directing of processing resources towards that thing. Directing processing resources towards something normally results in faster, more accurate processing of it" (2123).

is "a process of mental selection that is *within the control of the subject*," and need not concern action (535; emphasis mine).[12]

What is the role of attention in mental control? As noted in section 2, many see attention as the central mechanism of mental control: "If we have any mental control, it seems to start with our ability to influence our focus of attention ... To control our movements, our emotions, our addictions, our desires, our diets, or anything else, we must first control our attention" (Wegner 1988, 683). This reliance on attention has been described extensively in the case of self-control, which is part of mental control.[13] In the marshmallow task, for example, one strategy for overcoming temptation is to simply look away from the marshmallow, a form of "overt" attention (as opposed to "covert" attention, in which the eyes need not move). To move the eyes away from the marshmallow is to prioritize other stimuli over the marshmallow, potentially resulting in the selection of a thought process other than that of the tempting marshmallow. Further, it is this very skill of directing attention away from the distracting marshmallow that is thought to support subsequent academic success (Shoda, Mischel, and Peake 1990, 985). Later in development, self-control can be achieved either by directing attention away from temptations or by directing greater attention toward one's goals (Herdova 2017).

While attention supports self-control by altering the relative prioritization of otherwise salient stimuli, such as temptations, mental control goes beyond overcoming salient stimuli. Recall the ping-pong example from the prologue: mental control helps one to overcome distractions and temptations, but it also helps one to focus, to motivate, and to align mental processes, all of which can occur without the presence of distractions or temptations. Is attention required for all of these functions of mental control, or can mental control occur in some cases without the benefit of attention? Some separate control that depends on attention from "automatic" control. Arango-Muñoz and Bermúdez (2018), for example, distinguish two types of control: "One of them is reflective control – the often slow, effortful top-down control that we exert by recruiting working memory in novel or attention-demanding tasks. The other is intuitive or automatic control – the fast, rather effortless and intuitive control that we exert automatically, without the intervention of working memory" (90). Take, for instance, the direct selection of a response based on a stimulus, such as taking

---

[12] Within the sciences the issue shows up, for example, in clashes about whether attention modulates primary visual cortex (see, e.g., Mangun 1995 versus Posner and Gilbert 1999).

[13] Alexander (1910) provides an early instance of this claim from within philosophy: "If it should be admitted that there is direct voluntary control of the feelings and emotions, such restraint would be primarily due to attention" (291).

Table 3 Comparison of attention and stimulus-response pairings according to the criteria for mental control

Mental Control Criteria	Attention	Stimulus-Response Pairings
Control of the Mind	mental selection ✓	mental selection ✓
By the Mind	subject-level ✓	?

a drink when you see someone else doing so in a social setting: this automatic selection by stimulus-response pairings is arguably a form of control *of the mind*, but is it also *by the mind* (Table 3)?[14] I will briefly problematize this issue here before returning to it in subsection 3.3.

In order to determine whether mental control can occur without attention, we would first have to have good measures for when attention is present or absent. As indicated in the quote from Arango-Muñoz and Bermúdez, one way to tell whether or not attention is present is through the experience of *effort*. The child directing their attention away from the marshmallow will likely feel a sense of effort while doing so, as will the host who pays special attention to their dinner guest. As Metzinger puts it, "The conscious experience of actually initiating a shift of attention … involves a sense of effort" (Metzinger 2017, 26). Thus, in looking for mental control that occurs without attention we might look for *effortless* mental control.

Yet, the absence of effort does not always indicate the absence of attention, or even "executive" attention. In one study it was found that a patient had "preserved conscious executive control" but an "absence of any associated subjective feeling of mental effort" (Naccache et al. 2005, 1326). The patient had preserved function in anterior cingulate cortex – which is central to "executive attention" (Posner and Rothbart 1998) – as well as preserved functionality in the Stroop task, so the authors claim that "executive attention and conscious feeling of mental effort are dissociable" (1318). Similarly, Wu (2011) argues that attention, measured through eye movements or "saccades," can be goal oriented without making an impact on conscious experience: "One can, using an eye tracker, follow the path of an agent's saccades, and the resulting pattern is intelligibly dependent on the agent's goals … we are not aware of each of our saccades … This suggests that the shift of covert attention associated with each

---

[14] See, for example, the discussion of stimulus-response pairings in Du, Krakauer, and Haith 2022. While some may take these pairings to exhibit attention (see subsection 3.3), these are typically described as automatic pairings that occur without attention.

saccade does not involve any distinctive phenomenology" (98). Thus, we must supplement introspective and phenomenological methods with empirical ones if we are to determine the role of attention in mental control.

Yet, scientific methods have their own drawbacks when it comes to determining the role of attention in mental control. Measures of attention used by scientists often include executive control tasks, such as the Stroop test, "a test of selective attention" (Bench et al. 1993, 907; see also MacLeod and MacDonald 2000).[15] Given the overlap with executive control, these tasks are unlikely to help us much in distinguishing attention from mental control. Of course, there are other measures of attention, including visual search tasks, which have been used by scientists to tease apart, for example, attention and working memory (Kane et al. 2006). More work will be required to synthesize this empirical research along with the conceptual and phenomenological evidence in order to determine the line between attention and other forms of prioritization as well as the role of attention in mental control.

The authors discussed so far have made use of several different forms of attention. The difference between covert and overt attention was already mentioned, but readers may have noted other differences. For example, is the attention that can be grabbed by naturally salient stimuli the same attention that can be paid and that typically comes along with a feeling of effort? In the next subsection I delineate voluntary attention, the form most associated with mental control, and how it is tracked by scientists. I subsequently discuss skepticism about voluntary attention as mental control as well as the possibility of automatic mental control, and whether it occurs without attention.

3.1 Voluntary Attention

Recall the ping-pong example described earlier: mental control enables one to track the ping-pong ball, to initiate and maintain play, to inhibit distractors, to balance competing tasks, and perhaps to adjust one's body and environment for optimal play. All of these expressions of mental control can occur through attention, albeit different types of attention. *Spatial* attention can be used to track objects in space (Fiebelkorn, Pinsk, and Kastner 2018). An attention *set* allows one to initiate, switch, and maintain tasks (Stothart et al. 2019). *Selective* attention allows one to diminish the impact of distracting sights and sounds (Plebanek and Sloutsky 2017). *Split* attention can help one to engage in multiple tasks at the same time (Delvenne and Holt 2012). *Embodied* attention uses the

---

[15] While both WCST and Stroop can be used to detect attention disorders (see, e.g., Reeve and Schandler 2001), the former is less consistently related to attention (see, e.g., Somsen 2007).

body and surrounding space to improve performance (Abrams and Weidler 2015). These can all be seen as expressions of voluntary attention – voluntary attention to a spatial location, based on a specific target, by selecting the target from distractors, while splitting the available resources, or through bodily movements. There are many types of attention, many of which overlap, but it is voluntary attention in particular that is considered essential for mental control.

A commonly cited early source on attention is James' *Principles of Psychology*, which distinguishes "active and voluntary" attention from "passive, reflex, non-voluntary, effortless" attention (James 1890, 940). The former describes, for example, your attention to the ball while playing ping-pong, while the latter describes your attention to an unexpected sound that distracts you from play. One might think of voluntary attention as based in interests (i.e. the interest in winning the ping-pong game), and involuntary attention as based in naturally salient stimuli (i.e. unexpected sounds). James makes other distinctions – between "sensorial" and "intellectual" attention, on the one hand, and between "immediate" and "derived" attention, on the other – but these have not stood the test of time in quite the same way. Thus Ribot, a contemporary of James, claims that "there are two well-defined forms of attention: the one spontaneous, natural; the other voluntary, artificial" (Ribot 1890, 8).

Both James and Ribot saw voluntary attention as secondary to involuntary attention; Ribot hints at this in the preceding quotation. Yet, their work is sometimes summarized in a way that diminishes the importance of involuntary attention.[16] In fact, philosophers generally focus on voluntary attention at the expense of involuntary attention. For instance, around the same time as James and Ribot, Harris writes in a commentary on Kant: "Attention is self-activity, not a passivity of the mind. It is the will acting upon the intellect" (Harris 1881, 56). Kant was nonetheless aware of involuntary or "passive" attention, which he discusses in the context of observing beauty: "The object repeatedly arouses the attention, the mind being passive" (Kant 1951, 65).

Perhaps one reason philosophers and others have prioritized voluntary attention is because of its contributions to the "higher faculties" such as mental control. Harris, for example, follows the above quote limiting attention to voluntary attention with the claim that "the higher faculties ... all originate from the process of attention" (Harris 1881, 56). Voluntary attention might be described as a case of the mind controlling the mind (i.e. the mind's interests

---

[16] One can see this, for example, in a dissertation on attention written by a contemporaneous philosopher: "Plato's theory, the first reviewed in this research, and Ribot's, the last one examined, agree in one great particular ... attention is an effort, a motor effort in an organism and a sense of motor effort in consciousness" (Uhl 1890, 124).

dictating the distribution of its resources), while involuntary attention would thus be described as other forces controlling the mind (i.e. naturally salient stimuli dictating the distribution of the mind's resources). In the ping-pong example, your ability to play is disrupted by the unexpected sound; the sound grabs your attention away from your current interest, the game. The key to mental control is thus not simply attention, but voluntary attention, the fundamental form of mental control. By separating voluntary from involuntary attention, we can distinguish control of the mind *by the mind* from control of the mind *by the world*. Note that this idea depends on the separability of voluntary from involuntary attention. Yet, as with many mental functions, there are some ways in which voluntary and involuntary attention are separable, and other ways in which they are intertwined.

One way that we can separate voluntary from involuntary attention is through behavioral research on "endogenous" and "exogenous" attention (see, e.g., Posner 1980). This research is aimed at discovering the difference between the control of attention by the mind (*endo*genous) and the control of attention by the world (*exo*genous). This difference is measured by giving the research participant the task of detecting a target stimulus. Endogenous attention is brought about by a symbolic cue (e.g. an arrow) directing the research participant to the location of the subsequent target. Exogenous attention is instead triggered with a salient cue (e.g. a sudden flash at the location of the subsequent target). Findings from this research include that endogenous attention is slower to react to the cue but is sustained for a longer duration (Jonides 1981; Posner and Cohen 1984). Exogenous attention, on the other hand, reacts quickly to the cue but is then "inhibited" at that location. Thus, voluntary and involuntary attention have some functional and behavioral differences.

Research on endogenous and exogenous attention has in turn inspired neuroscientific research on "top-down" and "bottom-up" attention. The brain is sometimes seen in terms of a hierarchy, with sensory and motor areas at the bottom (e.g. occipital cortex; Figure 1a) and control areas at the top (e.g. prefrontal cortex; Figure 1e–i). Thus, bottom-up attention is prioritization that is primarily driven by sensory or motor activity, whereas top-down attention is prioritization that is primarily driven by control activity (e.g. the difference between the feedforward activity from primary visual areas depicted in Figure 1k–l and feedback from prefrontal cortex depicted in Figure 1j). This maps on reasonably well to the endogenous/exogenous distinction, such that the two distinctions are often treated as synonymous. Studies have found many differences between top-down and bottom-up attention, such as that top-down attention uses lower neural frequencies and bottom-up attention uses higher neural frequencies (Buschman and Miller 2007).[17] Thus, voluntary and involuntary attention also have some neuroscientific differences.

Despite these behavioral and neuroscientific differences, voluntary and involuntary attention are intertwined: "In the laboratory, exogenous and endogenous attention are studied predominantly in isolation, but in everyday life, they compete with one another" (Grubb et al. 2015, 438).[18] Consider the ping-pong example: someone whose voluntary attention is less engaged by the game will be more easily distracted by an unexpected sound, whereas someone whose voluntary attention is more engaged will be less easily distracted. Conversely, someone whose involuntary attention is activated by a distracting sound will likely find themselves unable to keep up their voluntary attention to the game, whereas someone whose involuntary attention is not activated will be able to continue as normal. Voluntary and involuntary attention seem connected, as though voluntary and involuntary are simply two types of inputs to a single system of attention. Yet, it is the contribution of voluntariness to this system that allows us to separate the subject-level mental selection we associate with attention from other forms of mental selection, such as selection via stimulus-response pairings.

That voluntary attention comes in degrees and that more such attention helps one to avoid distraction is an old idea. In 1886 *Mind* published an experimental study in which Cattell reported finding that attention comes in three "grades," and that a high grade of voluntary attention precludes distraction. This idea is supported by more recent work – Grubb et al. (2015) found that "focused endogenous attention can mitigate the impact of task-irrelevant exogenous onsets" and "can render negligible the exogenous impact of task-irrelevant onsets altogether once task performance has reached asymptotic levels" (443). On the other hand, distracting stimuli sometimes capture attention against one's wishes. As Tran puts it, "Rewarding stimuli can involuntarily capture attention in a visual search paradigm even when they directly conflict with current goals" (2020, 2). A standard example is that of sudden onset stimuli—such as when an object suddenly appears out of nowhere in your field of view—which reliably capture attention (Kawahara, Yanase, and Kitazaki 2012). Of course, there are cases in everyday life when even these types of stimuli are not distracting, such as when someone is wrapped up in a video game and waving one's hand in front of their face does not distract them from play (see also subsection 5.3). It may be

---

[17] "Neural frequencies" are the rates at which neurons fire. Thus, top-down attention occurs through slower firing rates than bottom-up attention. This difference in firing rate has been argued to contribute to the functional and behavioral differences (Jennings 2020a).

[18] For the opposing viewpoint, see, e.g., Prinzmetal et al. 2009; Rokem et al. 2010.

that it depends on the strength of voluntary attention, on the one hand, and the strength of the distracting stimulus, on the other.[19]

Many have suggested updating the distinction between voluntary and involuntary attention. Awh, Belopolsky, and Theeuwes, for example, suggest adding other influences, including the recent reward history of the subject: "We emphasize that priority is determined not just by goal- and stimulus-driven selection, but also by the lingering effects of past selection episodes (e.g., reward and selection history)" (2012, 438). This sort of change would not, of course, preclude the role of volition in attention, nor the value of voluntary attention for mental control. One recent review article, for instance, concludes from these criticisms that we should think of attention as "dynamically weighted prioritization, stipulating that multiple factors impinge onto the attentional priority map, each with a corresponding weight" (Shomstein, Zhang, and Dubbelde 2022). Other suggested updates go further, casting doubt on voluntary attention as the fundamental form of mental control, and in some cases on the actual existence of mental control. These more substantial criticisms are discussed in the next subsection.

3.2 Skepticism about Voluntary Attention as Mental Control

A common concern about mental control is that it forces us to import a "homunculus." In general, a homunculus is a model or copy of a human being at a smaller scale (it means "little person," in Latin). The brain is thought to have such a model in the sensory and motor cortices, with each area of the body represented according to either the sensitivity (sensory) or the dexterity (motor) of that area (the "sensorimotor homunculus"; e.g. Muret and Makin 2021). This version of the homunculus is not controversial, since it is passive. The controversial homunculus is active, enacting mental control through attention. Twenty years ago, for example, a major international symposium was held to "banish" the homunculus, "that conveniently intelligent but opaque agent still lurking within many theories, under the guise of a central executive or supervisory attentional system assumed to direct processes that are not 'automatic'" (Monsell and Driver 2000, i). What is the objection to the homunculus in this case? This has to do with the homunculus fallacy.

The homunculus fallacy is made when one introduces a homunculus to explain a mental phenomenon, such as perception or action. A memorable description of the problem comes from Skinner (1984):

---

[19] One way this issue has been explored in neuroscience is through causal interference with brain areas associated with voluntary attention: using transcranial magnetic stimulation to boost the frontal eye fields (FEF), for example, decreased the impact of distracting stimuli on a behavioral task (Lega et al. 2019).

It is tempting to attribute the visible behavior to another organism inside – to a little man or homunculus ... when a man's finger is pricked, electrical impulses resembling flashes of lightning run up the afferent nerves and appear on a television screen in the brain. The little man wakes up, sees the flashing screen, reaches out, and pulls a lever. More flashes of lightning go down the nerve to the muscles, which then contract, as the finger is pulled away from the threatening stimulus. The behavior of the homunculus was, of course, not explained. An explanation would presumably require another film. And it, in turn, another. (615)

Skinner cites the problem as one of *explanation*: the homunculus is used to explain the behavior of the organism, but it cannot have done so, because then the homunculus would require an explanation for its own behavior, leading to vicious regress. To return to our ping-pong example, one might ask: how are we able to perceive ping-pong paddles? We commit the homunculus fallacy if we respond: we perceive ping-pong paddles due to an inner perceiver, something inside of our heads that perceives the ping-pong paddles on our behalf (see Figure 2). This is a fallacy because if we do not have an explanation for how a person perceives ping-pong paddles then we cannot solve the problem by introducing an internal perceiver to take that person's place. After all, if we can only explain how a person perceives ping-pong paddles via an internal per-ceiver, then surely our explanation will have to include a ping-pong paddle perceiver for the internal perceiver, to explain how *it* perceives. Our explanation would not be complete, in fact, until we have supplied a ping-pong paddle perceiver for every ping-pong paddle perceiver – an unhappy consequence of this approach.

Figure 2 A depiction of a perceiving homunculus as conceived by the homunculus fallacy – the ping-pong paddle perceiver perceives in virtue of an inner ping-pong paddle perceiver

One problem driving the homunculus fallacy is of thinking that we must introduce an *internal agent* to account for mental activity. The activity of perceiving, for example, rather than simply reacting to stimuli, is thought to be something that should be explained. The homunculus is introduced to enable this activity, but according to its critics it has just shifted the explanation back a level. The problem is in introducing a perceiver when a perceiver is already available: the whole organism. Conversely, this aspect of the fallacy is dissolved if one denies the existence of a prior perceiver, taking the brain, or some part of the brain, to be the only available perceiver. That is, those who bring up this fallacy assume that the whole organism is the original perceiver, but one might object that the perceiver *just is* some part of the whole organism. In that case, a fallacy is not being committed, since no additional perceiver is being introduced in order to explain the fact of perception.

Another problem driving the homunculus fallacy is assuming that the source of mental activity must be localized, rather than distributed. The traditional perspective on self-control is to impute it to a dedicated mechanism or instrument. This "localized" approach might see a specific neural area, for example, as the seat of self-control. Compare this with trying to explain the emergence of a governed state from an anarchic one through the presence of a single elected official or government body. Such an explanation is unsatisfying on its own. One might ask, for example: How was that individual able to turn anarchy into order? One would have to account for both how they enabled the transition (e.g. the official came up with wise principles of social organization and was able to consistently apply them) and, likely, how other aspects of the state enabled the transition (e.g. the people admired the official and desired a more organized social environment). Similarly, if we want to understand mental activity, such as mental control, we need to find more than an agent who is responsible for the control; we must also find the way that the agent is able to exert control, and what about the mind supports the possibility of control.

In contrast to the traditional perspective is a distributed one. In connectionism, for example, mental functions are distributed across a neural network, rather than being attributable to a single part of the network. Self-control would thus arise out of many local interactions distributed across the brain, rather than occurring through a separable localized subsystem or controller (McClelland et al. 2010). This approach is partly inspired by the observation of substantial overlap and plasticity in the brain, which in turn puts pressure on the idea that mental functions, such as self-control, are natural kinds.

Some have thus argued that we should set aside the idea of a single agent or controller: "Until recently it seems to have been assumed that if control is exercised, then there must be a controller ... Yet the wide world also contains many examples of complex systems that are flexibly controlled without containing anything identifiable as a singular controller (e.g., termite communities)" (Monsell and Driver 2000, 4; see also Section 6). Supporting this alternative perspective is the fact that there is no single process or location in the brain that seems to enable control: "These processes, which can be collectively referred to as 'executive mechanisms of attentional control,' including the coordinated control over both input and output mechanisms, comprise several distinct operations with probably distinct anatomical substrates" (Robbins and Rogers 2000, 473). Thus, a popular view in the science of mind is that we should be skeptical about purported divisions between voluntary and involuntary, active and passive, controlled and automatic.[20] In their place, we should start with the assumption that we can explain the mind without such divisions, allowing for greater continuity with the natural world and explanations of other scientific phenomena.

While a distributed, systems approach to cognition is popular today, similar issues came up over one hundred years ago in a debate between James (1890) and Bradley (1886). Bradley was an idealist and so preferred continuity in his explanations of mental and other phenomena (much like current day physicalists); he argued that both active and passive attention came down to interest on the part of the subject, and thus that both could be reduced to mere interests (Bradley 1886; Jennings 2020a, 41; see also Mole 2017).[21] For example, while we may want to distinguish the effortful attention one gives to a difficult text from the effortless attention one gives to a distracting sound, Bradley claims that in both cases attention is directed to the stimulus simply due to the interests of the subject – an overriding interest in the text in one case and an overriding interest in the sound in the other. The sense of effort that distinguishes them must then be an illusion. Unlike Bradley, James was open to explanatory discontinuity and the possibility of mental activity as distinct from physical passivity.[22] He thus made much of the distinction between voluntary and involuntary attention, seeing attention as the foundation of volition and mental control. Yet, James found that the empirical evidence available in his time was inadequate to decide between his view and Bradley's.

---

[20] This idea is also present in the work of some philosophers. Ganeri, for example, suggests that we replace the voluntary/involuntary distinction with other ways of understanding attention drawn from Indian philosophy (2017).

[21] In basic terms, while most scientists believe that everything is physical (physicalism; Stoljar 2017), some philosophers believe that everything is mental or based in the mental (idealism). Both positions are a form of *monism*: the view that there is one fundamental substrate of reality (Robinson 2020).

[22] James is a famous advocate of *neutral monism*, the view that there is a single fundamental substrate of reality that it is neither mental nor physical, yet the mental and the physical are two ways of conceptualizing this underlying substrate (Stubenberg 2018).

Since the time of that debate, some contemporary evidence has arisen to challenge the idea that mental control is the right way of thinking about the role of attention in the mind. Much of this work has been connected to Wegner, who argues that mental control is an illusion. In an early publication on the topic, he and Schneider cite James as background before casting doubt on the effectiveness of mental control (1989). They review, for example, their work on the "white bear" study, in which they asked participants not to think of a white bear: "These subjects showed a level of thinking about a white bear … significantly greater than that shown by subjects in a comparison group who were asked from the start (immediately after the practice period) to think about a white bear" (297). They thus reason that mental control is ineffective (see also Wegner 1994; Hohwy 2004). Yet, as Nahmias has pointed out, this evidence seems to support the view that mental control *is* effective in some way, in the sense that it has a measurable effect on the mind, albeit an unintended one (2002).

Wegner's later work goes further: "Experiences of conscious will thus arise from processes whereby the mind interprets itself – not from processes whereby mind creates action. Conscious will, in this view, is an indication that we think we have caused an action, not a revelation of the causal sequence by which the action was produced" (2004, 649). In other words, we infer the presence of mental control due to various factors (e.g. congruity between our current thoughts and behavior); but this does not mean that mental control is a real phenomenon. That we experience ourselves as exerting mental control in acts of attention does not mean that we actually exert mental control in such cases. This conclusion is based in part on studies finding that participants can be tricked into thinking that they caused an action if the conditions are right (Wegner and Wheatley 1999). For example, participants can be tricked into thinking that they played a larger role than a confederate in bringing about an action (when in fact the confederate played a larger role) if they are primed with a thought that is congruous with the action just before that action. Since participants can be tricked in this way, Wegner reasons that mental control is an illusion. That is, he reasons that we do not actually exert mental control, even though it seems to us that we do.

While Wegner's work is compelling, it does not definitively establish that mental control is an illusion in this way. We know, of course, that even real phenomena can sometimes have illusory aspects. We have all been fooled into thinking the moon takes up a larger chunk of the visual field at the horizon than when it is higher in the sky (the "moon illusion"), yet this should not lead us to think that the moon itself is an illusion – only its apparent size is, in certain conditions. Similarly, it may be that we can be tricked as to the extent of our role in a particular behavior or outcome, but this does not mean that we play no such role. In other words, rather than concluding that we do not actually exert mental control, one might conclude that we can be confused as to the extent of control that we exert.

Some have used scientific evidence to dispute Wegner's claims, including "hard evidence that conscious intentions (or their physical correlates) sometimes *are* among the causes of corresponding actions ... from research on implementation intentions" (Mele 2018, 7; see also Mele 2009) as well as broader findings on "the activity involved in deliberating, deciding, forming prior intentions, and carrying out extended actions" (Nahmias 2002). Velmans (2002) specifically calls out attention as effective in mental control as it enables patients to manage pain: "In clinical practice, the effects of imagery on brain, body and other conscious experience are often explained to patients in terms of *refocusing and redirection of attention*" (8; emphasis in the original). Yet, even if there is evidence in favor of the effectiveness of mental control in certain cases, Wegner's work does cast doubt on the view that mental control is all that it seems. Thus, a complete account of mental control will need to explain the cases in which it goes astray.

Beyond this empirical work, philosophical work since the time of James and Bradley has also cast doubt on the possibility of mental control, at least as separable from physical control. The work of Kim, especially, has challenged the popular conception of mental causation, which is relevant to this discussion insofar as mental control is seen as a form of mental causation (e.g. Kim 2007). As Kim argues, the causal closure of the physical, or the assumption that every physical event has a sufficient physical cause, prevents the existence of a separable causal power (but see Bennett 2003). This includes causal power in a mind that is separable from the physical substrate of that mind. Kim argued that even "supervenience" theories, in which the mind "supervenes" on its physical substrate, fail this causal closure test. In supervenience theories the mind is separate from the physical substrate in that the substrate can change without corresponding changes in the mind (allowing for multiple realization), but any change in the mind will depend on changes in the physical substrate.[23] In such a scenario Kim argues that the only way to maintain causal closure of the physical is to allow for massive overdetermination, such that the relevant physical events (P*) have both a mental cause (M) and a physical cause (P): "The fact of the matter is that there is only one causal process here, from P to P*, and M's supposed causal contribution to the production of P* is totally mysterious" (Kim 2007, 48).

---

[23] As McLaughlin and Bennett (2021) put it: "*A*-properties supervene on *B*-properties if and only if a difference in *A*-properties *requires* a difference in *B*-properties," wherein "requires" can have different modal strengths.

If Kim's reasoning is correct, we would need to discard one of the following: (a) the causal closure of the physical, in which every physical event has a sufficient physical cause; (b) mental causation; or (c) the separability of the mind from its physical substrate. An epiphenomenalist (one who does not endorse mental causation) could adopt (a) and (c), and a physicalist (one who endorses the reducibility of the mental to the physical) could adopt (a) and (b). But a supervenience theorist who wants to maintain this type of mental control would have to discard (a), causal closure. As Kim puts it, "Within a physicalist scheme, mental causation is possible only if mental phenomena are physically reducible" (2007, 1).[24]

Many have taken these arguments to show that mental causation is inoperable but have tried to find noncausal roles for the mind. Mascolo and Kallio (2019), for example, argue in favor of a self-regulation account of agency, in which "existing capacities for biological control are transformed by the embodied emergence of meaning and experience" (455). In their view, the emergence of meaning and experience allows for self-representation, which then influences existing systems of self-regulation in a noncausal way (see also subsection 6.2). Others have argued that mental causation can be rescued through a denial of local supervenience (Baker 2009; Jennings 2020a; Jennings 2020b). Contextual emergence, for example, denies local but not global supervenience, such that a mental cause may depend on a supervenience base that goes beyond the physical makeup of the body. Thus, one can hold onto the (global) causal closure of the physical and the separability of the mental from its local physical substrate while also believing in mental causation through mental control. This form of emergence will be discussed at more length in Section 6.

3.3 The Possibility of Automatic Mental Control

We have so far focused on the connection between attention and mental control. It is common in psychology textbooks to list both as opposed to automaticity. As one textbook puts it, "This distinction between automatic and intentional (attentional, controlled) processes is fundamental to many domains in psychology" (Balota and Marsh 2004, 183; see also Posner and Snyder 2004). Thus, Proust (2001) claims that automatic attention "is not genuine attention" (112). Of course, there are multiple characteristics and forms of automaticity; automaticity can be opposed to consciousness, intention, attention, and control (Moors and Houwer 2007). This particular opposition concerns whether a process is

---

[24] This is not to say that mental phenomena would be *epistemically* reducible. It may be the case, for example, that it is best to *describe* mental causation at the mental level even if it is metaphysically reducible to the physical level (see, e.g., Campbell 2010).

sensitive to the agent's current goals and intentions. Attention and mental control are sensitive to the agent's current goals and intentions, but automatic processes are assumed not to be: "Automatic/controlled processing theory assumes that human performance is the result of two qualitatively different processes" (Schneider, Dumais, and Shiffrin 1982, 1).

The common assumption is that a process cannot be both controlled and automatic in the same way at the same time, and thus that a process benefiting from attention and mental control cannot be *purely* automatic, or entirely insensitive to one's goals and intentions. Yet, most processes use some combination of control and automaticity, and so one might call a process relatively controlled or relatively automatic (see, e.g., Pacherie and Mylopoulos 2021). Many have argued that the automatic components of a process can be chunked for greater control, as is seen in skilled behavior (see, e.g., Dayer and Jennings 2021). That is, once one part of a skilled behavior becomes habitual, one can allow that part of the skilled behavior to proceed automatically, opening up control resources for other parts of the skilled behavior. In this case the overall process would still be relatively controlled and so would not count as automatic.

Yet, some philosophers have argued that this perspective is mistaken. These philosophers argue for the existence of automatic attention and automatic mental control. Two philosophers that are especially prominent in this discussion are Wu and Fridland. Fridland, for example, lists "automatic attention" as one of three types of control, citing Wu as inspiration for her view (Fridland 2014). Fridland's reasoning in this paper is based on evidence that agents might not be able to report what they are attending to or might not direct their attention through conscious intention: "Skilled hockey players, for example, do not have to tell themselves to attend to the initial segment of the puck's trajectory. Rather, selective attention is deployed automatically, once the trained agent initiates intentional action" (Fridland 2014, 2746). But whether or not attention is deployed *consciously* does not tell us about the process and whether it is sensitive to the agent's current goals and intentions. Thus, this evidence is not enough to conclude that there is automatic mental control in the sense mentioned above.

Similarly, Wu (2016) makes the case for automatic attention through an experiment by Yarbus: "Yarbus asked his subjects to visually examine a painting and to perform several tasks … What is striking is that the pattern of eye movements is intelligible given the subject's goals" (110). Wu argues that these specific eye patterns were not intended by the participants in this study and so were automatic. But, again, automaticity in the view of this discussion has to do with an absence of sensitivity to the agent's current goals and intentions, not merely an absence of conscious intention. If those eye movements are sensitive to the agent's current goals and intentions then they are not automatic, on this view.

A different reason some argue for the possibility of automatic mental control hinges on the role of external cues. Take, for example, a coach's encouragement to push through resistance during a difficult physical exercise: the idea is that this cue can cause an automatic form of mental control. Namely, since familiar external cues can lead to automatic response, if we take those cues to sometimes support mental control then they might count as a form of automatic mental control. This reasoning is provided by, for example, Mann and Ward, who find that control is sometimes increased even while attention is decreased (2007). They argue this occurs when there are salient cues that support a controlled behavior; the loss of attention leads to better capture by those salient cues and thus less distraction by temptations. For example, antismoking messaging that is normally ineffective at curbing smoking *is* effective when the smokers are engaged in an attention-demanding task. As Mann and Ward put it: "Our preliminary findings suggest a U-shaped relationship between attention and self-control. Self-control appears to be most successful both at times when attention is fully available to devote to the relevant self-control task and at times when attention is so focused on a competing task that no notice is taken of temptations that may lead to a loss of control" (2007, 283). That is, when attention is focused on a competing task *and* salient cues support the controlled behavior then no notice is taken of surrounding temptations.

Against Mann and Ward's proposal, one might argue that control by salient environmental cues is not mental control at all. Instead, it is a kind of "lucky" or accidental control, since it is lucky that one has been captured by cues that are beneficial toward one's goals. Recall that mental control is not just control *of* the mind, or control that is consistent with one's goals, but control *by* the mind. Thus, this form of automatic control by external cues does not appear to be a candidate for automatic mental control.

A similar idea to that of Mann and Ward is proposed by Vierkant (2014), who argues that willpower has two components, one of which is automatic. He compares this automatic component to Odysseus' tying himself to the mast to avoid the temptation of the sirens: "Willpower itself has, as it were, a tying part and a tied part. Willpower achieves self control by performing an intentional action (the tying) that leads to a cognitive environment that prevents re-evaluation" (63). So the automatic part of mental control would be the follow-through for a nonautomatic intention.

While intuitive, it is not yet clear if Vierkant's idea is supported by empirical evidence. Take, for example, the empirical work on "goal shielding." Goal shielding is the inhibition of competing goals in order to complete a task, such as the (temporary!) inhibition of cleaning goals in favor of writing goals. Shah, Friedman, and Kruglanski (2002) found that goal shielding occurs for subliminal goals, demonstrating that goal shielding can be "automatic": "This represents the first experimental evidence for the automaticity of goal shielding" (1267). Since goal shielding is the inhibition of competing goals in order to complete a task, this may be taken as evidence that mental control can be automatic, in keeping with Vierkant. Yet, Shah, Friedman, and Kruglanski only show that goal shielding is automatic in the sense that it can be activated *subconsciously*, finding the application of goal shielding to be highly sensitive to "(a) the characteristics of the goals themselves, and (b) to the motivational and emotional context in which the self-regulatory activity is unfolding" (1262). While automatic processes can be sensitive to context, as the authors note, these specific types of sensitivities leave it ambiguous as to whether goal shielding is automatic in the relevant sense. That is, if goal shielding is sensitive to the subject's goals and motivations, it does not appear to be at all like the case of Odysseus tying himself to the mast: Odysseus' plan would have failed if his knots loosened with changes in his goals and motivations, as when he hears the siren's song. Thus, goal shielding has not yet provided evidence of automatic control in the sense required here (i.e. insensitive to the subject's goals and intentions).

This section has reviewed the centrality of attention, and especially voluntary attention, in mental control, as well as questioning some objections and challenges to this characterization of mental control. The next section covers meditation and mind wandering, typically thought to be at two ends of the spectrum with respect to attention and mental control. It provides evidence supporting the view that meditation is exemplary mental control, while challenging the idea that mind wandering is necessarily opposed to it. That is, while mind wandering does normally occur during lapses of mental control, it can co-opt some of its essential mechanisms. For that reason, I have separated the discussion of mind wandering from that of ADHD, a more straightforward disorder of control covered in Section 5.

4 Meditation and Mind Wandering

Meditation and mind wandering are typically seen as occupying two ends of the mental control spectrum, with meditation serving as an exemplary form of mental control and mind wandering exhibiting its absence. Yet, recent work on these phenomena has challenged this perspective: some argue that meditation can occur without mental control, while others argue that mind wandering sometimes embodies mental control. After reviewing the evidence I find no reason to reject the traditional perspective on meditation as a form of mental control but agree that mind wandering is an orthogonal phenomenon, sometimes occurring with the benefit of mental control and sometimes occurring without it.

4.1 Meditation

Meditation includes a collection of practices that all aim to control and direct the mind in some way. A commonly discussed form is "mindfulness" meditation, "non-judgemental attention to present-moment experiences" (Tang, Holzel, and Posner 2015, 1). One might use this form of meditation in everyday activities, such as while walking or washing the dishes: the process is meditative so long as one stays in the present moment, without evaluation or reflection. In contrast, "focused attention" meditation (FAM) specifically requires that one focus on a particular part or aspect of one's experience, while "open awareness" meditation (OAM) requires that one *not* focus on any part or aspect of one's experience (Upton and Brent 2019, 58).[25] A traditional form of FAM requires the subject to sit in a quiet location and focus on her breath, whereas in OAM she may simply stay present without an explicit object of focus by noticing whatever is happening around her. Attention is a central mechanism for all three forms of meditation: while Tang, Holzel, and Posner (2015) describe mindfulness meditation as attention to awareness, in general, Upton and Brent (2019) describe FAM as increasing attentional focus, whereas OAM removes attentional focus. Thus, these latter forms of meditation both have to do with the control of attentional focus.

The practice of meditation has been found to lead to improvements in attention and mental control. Attention is typically subject to "attentional blink," in which attending to a target causes the subject to miss subsequent targets within a certain time frame, almost as though the subject had blinked. Meditation decreases the duration of attentional blink, which some say leads to "enhanced phenomenology" for meditators (Latham 2016, 1795). Along those lines, meditators have been found to have greater introspective accuracy in certain cases (e.g. greater accuracy in reports of perceived tactile sensitivity, in comparison to objective sensitivity; Fox et al. 2012). More relevant for mental control is that meditation leads to improvements in sustained attention, especially for experienced meditators (Valentine and Sweet 1999). The improved ability to sustain attention in meditation has been linked to prefrontal cortex, in

---

[25] Some consider mindfulness meditation to include FAM and OAM as types (see, e.g., Tang, Holzel, and Posner 2015), but I will treat these forms as separable.

line with the view of mental control and attention described in subsection 3.1 (Lippelt, Hommel, and Colzato 2014).

Different types of meditation have been found to improve different aspects of mental control. Mindfulness meditation, for example, was found in one study to improve sustained attention but not performance on tasks that require inhibition, such as Stroop tasks (Semple 2010). In contrast, both FAM and OAM have been found to improve the inhibitory capacities of executive attention: "Both FA and OM practice had a selective, rather than global effect on attention; specifically involving those mechanisms involved in the resolution of cognitive conflict between task relevant and task irrelevant/distractor stimuli" (Ainsworth et al. 2013, 1229–1230).[26] Thus, while all forms of meditation appear to support mental control, they may not support every type of mental control.

Despite a strong association with attention and mental control, some object to the above account of meditation, at least for expert meditators. Lutz et al. (2008), for example, describe this position:

> Traditional Buddhist scholars have emphasized the decreased need for voluntary attentional efforts to attain concentration following expertise in FA meditation. In addition, some variations of OM meditation advise practitioners to drop any explicit effort to control the occurrence of thoughts or emotions to further stabilize their meditation. These descriptions suggest that some meditation states might not be best understood as top-down influences in a classical neuroanatomical sense but rather as dynamical global states that, in virtue of their dynamical equilibrium, can influence the processing of the brain from moment to moment. (166–167)

That is, expert meditators claim that FAM requires little to no voluntary attention over time and that OAM feels effortless. Further, Lutz et al. think that we might explain this through "large-scale coherent neuronal ensembles" that have an impact on local processing, rather than through specific neural areas, such as prefrontal cortex. One might conclude from this that meditation need not use attention or mental control, against the perspective provided above. Yet, there is an alternative explanation of all three of these points.

First, that FAM is reported to require less attention over time is consistent with the literature on skilled behavior, wherein skill lessens the requirement of attention. That is, skill depends on habitual behaviors that become more automatic over time, relying on stimulus-response pairings in place of attentional oversight (see Section 3). But many have noted that skilled behavior nonetheless *typically* combines both habitual and attention-involving elements.

---

[26] Mindfulness meditation and OAM are sometimes seen as synonymous, which might make these results seem contradictory. Ainsworth et al. (2013) specify that OAM often begins with focus before attention is intentionally broadened, which may help lead to this effect.

Dayer and Jennings (2021), for example, summarize research on how attention occurs at different spatiotemporal grains for experts as they gain in skill: an expert ping-pong player may no longer use attention to respond to every serve, instead using attention to monitor broader issues of game play. Moreover, attention is used at different points in the time course of skill deployment: an expert ping-pong player may be able to play an entire game on autopilot, but they likely use attention to both enter and leave that automatic state. Thus, we might expect that FAM requires less attention over time while nonetheless typically making use of voluntary attention, at least at some points in its time course.

Second, it may be that for both FAM and OAM mental control only *seems* to be absent due to a lack of felt effort, which may itself be absent due to meditation's greater reliance on ventromedial prefrontal cortex (vmPFC), rather than dorsolateral prefrontal cortex (dlPFC). That is, neural areas that correspond with mental control include lateral and medial prefrontal areas, such as dlPFC (Figure 1g) and vmPFC (Figure 1i). The traditional way of thinking about the different roles of vmPFC and dlPFC is in terms of "hot" and "cold" executive functions: "The vmPFC is assumed to have a crucial role in emotional processing, whereas the dlPFC is predominantly involved in cognitive control and executive processing" (Nejati et al. 2021, 1). In fact, both play a role in cognitive control and emotional cognition. A better way of thinking about their separable roles for our purposes is that dlPFC is responsible for *switching* attention (e.g. Rossi et al. 2009) whereas vmPFC aids in *sustaining* attention by inhibiting distractors (e.g. Broersen and Uylings 1999; Kahn et al. 2012). Some have described this difference in terms of exploring an environment (dlPFC) versus exploiting one aspect of the environment (vmPFC; Laureiro-Martínez et al. 2015; see also Sripada 2018; Domenech, Rheims, and Koechlin 2020). Regardless, dlPFC is the area associated with feelings of effort (Soutschek and Tobler 2020), while vmPFC is the area that sees an increase in activity during meditation and that is associated with sustained attention (Lutz et al. 2004; Chau et al. 2018).

Take, for example, a study on the ability of expert meditators to suppress a particular neural area, posterior cingulate cortex (PCC) (Garrison et al. 2013). This neural area is part of the default mode network (DMN) and is associated with mind wandering.[27] Garrison et al. found that expert meditators did not have an active PCC during so-called "effortless" meditation, but did have an active PCC in "distracted" meditation, and that they were able to volitionally

---

[27] The DMN is a collection of brain areas, such as vmPFC and hippocampus, that are hypothesized to be most active when the brain is not engaged in a task (see, e.g., Raichle 2015).

deactivate PCC through neural feedback.[28] A natural description of this research is that these experts were sometimes interrupted by mind wandering during their meditation practice but were able to get back on track by suppressing that mind wandering. Given the volitional nature of the process, as described by the authors, this would be a clear case of mental control. While the authors did not track neural areas other than PCC, we can map this onto the discussion above by imagining that vmPFC supported sustained attention in the effortless case, but that the inhibitory faculties of dlPFC helped to suppress PCC activity in the distracted, effortful case.

It is worth noting that the connections between vmPFC and other areas are different in experienced meditators. In one study, vmPFC in experienced meditators had decreased connections to areas associated with self-reference but increased connections to other areas (Taylor et al. 2013). This too might explain the difference in perceived mental control. That is, meditation may be less likely to activate neural areas associated with self-reference, even while it makes use of mental control.

Third, and finally, one may think, following the quote from Lutz et al. (2008) earlier, that a dynamical account of meditation necessarily replaces the view that meditation makes use of mental control and voluntary attention. To the contrary, this Element provides a dynamical account of mental control and voluntary attention. That mental control uses macrolevel neural ensembles is not inconsistent with there being particular neural regions that tend to support such ensembles (such as dlPFC and vmPFC), nor with the idea that this process should be described as an instance of voluntary attention. This "wave dynamics" approach is discussed at more length below as well as in Sections 5 and 6.

4.2 Mind Wandering

Let's return to the ping-pong example. So far we have explained how one might use mental control to improve play – to focus on the ball over time in the face of other tasks and distractions. Imagine that it is a warm summer's day and you are outside with three of your best friends, one across the table ready to serve and two conversing nearby. You overhear in their conversation "remember Albuquerque?" before a peal of laughter. And you do remember: You remember trying to recreate scenes from the hit television show *Breaking Bad* with your friends and how ridiculous you all looked trying to do it. But your friend across

---

[28] In contrast, a recently published paper asserts that effortless meditation actually makes use of PCC: "Based on the existing literature, we propose the ACC [anterior cingulate cortex], PCC, and striatum as key neural correlates of effortless training" (Tang et al. 2022, 8).

the table has just served and you were not ready, because you were remembering Albuquerque. You allowed your mind to wander.

As with attention, the definition of mind wandering is unsettled. Exemplar cases are those in which mental control lapses during a task, as in the ping-pong example above. Whereas mental control is intentional, mind wandering is typically defined as unintentional. Whereas mental control maintains a task, mind wandering is typically defined as "off-task." Whereas mental control is focused, mind wandering is typically defined as meandering. Yet, these exemplar qualities do not capture all cases of mind wandering, since mind wandering can arguably be intentional, on-task, and even focused. For this reason, competing accounts of mind wandering have emerged.

Contemporary debates on the relationship between mind wandering and mental control begin with Smallwood and Schooler (2006), who see mental control as a key element of mind wandering: "Mind wandering involves both the redirection of executive control and a failure of goal-oriented processing toward the primary task. In mind wandering, it seems that the automatic activation of a pertinent personal goal temporarily overshadows the more immediate goal of task completion" (956). Rather than seeing mind wandering as the absence of control, Smallwood and Schooler see it as mental control that has been redirected without intention or awareness. That is, it has been directed away from the primary task and toward a "personal" one. Take the ping-pong example above: Your mind went from being focused on the ping-pong game, your primary task, to being focused on your memories of Albuquerque, your personal task. This account can explain why mind wandering is prevalent when performance does not require mental control (since these resources can then be directed toward mind wandering) and why mind wandering harms performance that requires mental control (because it has been redirected). Smallwood et al. argue in a later paper that attention tends to oscillate between external (e.g. ping-pong) and internal (e.g. memory) tasks: "Our data suggest that when trying to engage attention in a sustained manner, the mind will naturally ebb and flow in the depth of cognitive analysis it applies to events in the external environment" (2008, 458).

In contrast with this account is that of McVay and Kane (2010), who reject the idea that mind wandering is a form of internally directed mental control: "The main difference between our perspective and that of Smallwood and Schooler concerns the relation between mind wandering and executive resources: They argued that mind wandering requires executive resources, whereas we argue that mind wandering results from executive-control failure" (189). They reason that mind wandering occurs when mental control is unsuccessful, using as evidence cases in which mind wandering increases in the absence of mental control *capacity*. Within individuals, fatigue and alcohol use both reduce mental control capacity and lead to more mind wandering. Across individuals, those with attention disorders (ADHD) mind wander more, whereas those with high working memory capacities mind wander less (see, e.g., McVay, Kane, and Kwapil 2009; Kane and McVay 2012). Thus, McVay and Kane reason that mind wandering occurs not when mental control is directed toward an internal task but when "automatically generated, personal-goal related thoughts" manage to defeat the ability of "the executive-control system to defend primary-task performance against interference from these thoughts" (199). In other words, mind wandering reflects the overturning, not redirecting, of mental control.

In light of the evidence presented by McVay and Kane (2010), Smallwood and Schooler presented an updated account, which they dub the "context regulation hypothesis" (2015). In this account, those with good functioning mental control (i.e. in the absence of fatigue, alcohol, ADHD, etc.) can suppress mind wandering when the task requires it but will engage mind wandering when task demands are low (see also Shepherd 2019). Thus, in the context of a demanding task mind wandering will be low, but in the context of no task or an undemanding task mind wandering will be high: "These results suggest that effective executive control can suppress self-generated thought when external demands are high; however, when demands of the task are low, executive control will take advantage of the person's excess resources and indulge in mind wandering" (506). This updated account makes room for the advantages gained by mind wandering in the appropriate circumstances (e.g. creativity), which is left out by an account that focuses on mind wandering as failure.

Neural evidence is sometimes used to support Smallwood and Schooler's (2015) account. Namely, recall that dlPFC and vmPFC are prefrontal neural areas that correspond with mental control. If these areas play a role in mind wandering then it would seem that mental control is a key element in mind wandering. As it happens, the year of Smallwood and Schooler's updated account saw the widely cited publication of the claim that stimulation of dlPFC increases episodes of mind wandering (Axelrod et al. 2015). Similarly, damage to the vmPFC was soon after claimed to decrease mind wandering: "Despite using different methodologies, Axelrod et al.'s (2015) study and ours converge in showing that prefrontal cortex regions are crucial for mind-wandering" (Bertossi and Ciaramelli 2016, 1788).

Integrating this neural evidence, Irving and Glasser suggest redefining mind wandering as "unguided attention" (2020; see also Irving 2016; Christoff et al. 2016). They review previous attempts at a definition and find that these definitions fail to capture certain cases of mind wandering. Recall the exemplar characteristics of mind wandering: unintentional, off-task, and meandering.

Irving and Glasser find the third of these to be the most important, suggesting a "dynamic" account of mind wandering. Previous accounts were centered on the first two characteristics, but Irving and Glasser argue that these "static" accounts fail to make important distinctions (i.e. between mind wandering and rumination) or to capture important cases (i.e. task-related mind wandering). In their account, mind wandering lacks regulatory control (also called "attentional guidance") and so is allowed to meander. They flesh out this account in neural terms, saying that mind wandering occurs when the DMN is unconstrained or unguided. This network includes the hippocampus and vmPFC, described earlier, both of which have been found to play an important role in mind wandering: "The vmPFC is critical for the initiation of endogenous spontaneous thought and the hippocampus for its form and content" (McCormick et al. 2018, 2752).

One might gather from the above that mental control is a key element of mind wandering, due to the apparent involvement of both attention (according to Irving and Glasser) and neural areas associated with mental control (i.e. prefrontal areas). Yet, questions remain. Recall that alcohol, which reduces the power of dlPFC, was found to increase mind wandering (Loheswaran et al. 2018). Similarly, fatigue corresponds with both reduced dlPFC activity and increased mind wandering (Soutschek and Tobler 2020). In contrast, according to Axelrod et al. (2015), *stimulation* of dlPFC leads to more mind wandering. In Irving and Glasser's (2020) account, only vmPFC and hippocampus play a role in mind wandering, so where does that leave dlPFC?

One reason to leave out dlPFC in an account of mind wandering is that the Axelrod et al. results were not replicated in a recent study by a separate group: "In a high-powered, preregistered multicentre study, we were not only unable to detect an effect of anodal transcranial direct current stimulation on mind-wandering propensity, but we actually found evidence for the absence of such an effect" (Boayue et al. 2020, 774).[29] In fact, the authors of the replication effort found that the Axelrod et al. results could have derived from mPFC, which include vmPFC: "We argue that stimulation of the MPFC could just as well be responsible for the effect reported by Axelrod et al. (2015) than that of the left DLPFC" (Boayue et al. 2020, 773). Thus, the seemingly contradictory nature of these claims may not need reconciliation after all.

As for vmPFC, one way of explaining how vmPFC both sustains attention and allows for mind wandering is through wave dynamics. As background, note that the brain is made up of gray matter, or neurons, and white matter that

---

[29] See also Csifcsák et al. 2019; Chaieb et al. 2019.

connects those neurons. Cognition is presumed to take place primarily in the interactions between neurons. These interactions can include, for example, electrical signals (e.g. action potentials), chemical signals (e.g. neurotransmitters), and field effects (e.g. local field potentials). Neural correlates can thus include, for example, areas of the brain (e.g. V1), neurochemicals (e.g. dopamine), and oscillatory frequencies (e.g. alpha waves). To say that we can understand the relationship between sustained attention and mind wandering through wave dynamics is to say that we can understand this relationship through features of the oscillatory activity of the neurons in these brain areas (see also Section 6). Recall that Smallwood et al. (2008) found sustained attention to naturally "ebb and flow." This fits naturally within a wave dynamics model, since waves likewise ebb and flow. What is more, changes in sustained attention have been found to correspond with neural oscillations (Clayton, Yeung, and Kadosh 2015). Spontaneous neural signals associated with mind wandering will have a chance of interrupting sustained attention either in the troughs of the oscillations or when the oscillations have less power. Those spontaneous neural signals might correspond with distracting external stimuli or with distracting internal thoughts. In either case the signals can hijack attention away from the primary task. In the case of distracting internal thoughts, this paves the way for mind wandering.

In sum, mind wandering can be defined as unguided thinking, with its prevalence predicted by Smallwood and Schooler's (2015) context regulation hypothesis. It has been found to occur when the control network (including dlPFC) no longer exerts top-down constraints on the DMN (including vmPFC and hippocampus), or when its top-down constraints are weak. In that case, a neural area that typically supports attention to the task (vmPFC) is redirected to internal processing, which some call "internal attention" (Chun, Golomb, and Turk-Browne 2011). It may do this, for example, by suppressing neural activity that conflicts with mind wandering. But it may also be the case that mind wandering is possible in the absence of this support from vmPFC (as in those who have damage to vmPFC – "vmPFC patients"). That is, it may be that only sustained mind wandering requires vmPFC: "vmPFC patients' mind-wandering ... seem to depend critically on the presence of external cues" (Ciaramelli and Treves 2019, 2).

Thus, mind wandering is not clearly opposed to mental control, at least not in all cases. It can reflect a failure of mental control in certain cases, while in others it can reflect excess cognitive resources that need not be directed to the main task. The fact that sustained mind wandering recruits areas of the brain key to mental control (i.e. vmPFC) further speaks to its integration with, rather than opposition to, mental control.

In the next section I look at a disorder of attention and mental control: ADHD. As I will try to show, this disorder sheds further light on mental control and how it works in the brain.

5 Attention Deficit Hyperactivity Disorder

As was discussed in earlier sections through the ping-pong example, mental control has many different aspects and functions, each of which can be understood through attention: the initiation and maintenance of a preferred activity, focus on stimuli relevant to that activity, inhibiting distractors irrelevant to that activity, situating the body and motor system to take part in that activity, and coordinating the preferred activity with other activities (see subsection 3.1). Any of these functions can fail, leading to a disorder of attention and control. In this section I will discuss one of the most significant of such disorders and how it relates to these different functions, while also noting potential advantages of the disorder with regard to other functions.

5.1 Defining the Disorder

Perhaps the most significant disorder of mental control is ADHD. As the name indicates, the main components of this heterogenous disorder are inattention and hyperactivity/impulsivity, with three disorder subtypes: primarily inattentive, primarily hyperactive/impulsive, and a combination of inattentive and hyperactive/impulsive (see, e.g., Setyawan et al. 2018). The description of inattention used by clinicians includes failures of selective attention ("often fails to give close attention to details or makes careless mistakes"), sustained attention ("has difficulty sustaining attention"), inhibition ("easily distracted by extraneous stimuli"), and task coordination ("has difficulty organizing tasks and activities"; Substance Abuse and Mental Health Services Administration 2016, 17). Hyperactivity includes gross motor ("runs about or climbs in situations where it is inappropriate"), fine motor ("fidgets with or taps hands or feet"), and verbal activity ("talks excessively"), whereas impulsivity is primarily social ("interrupts or intrudes on others"; see also Pappas 2006). From these descriptions it is clear that ADHD is age relative, at least in childhood. For that reason, some have argued that it is an "extreme end of a normal psychological trait" (Barkley 1997, 20).

As one of the most common behavioral disorders, ADHD affects around 5 percent of the population worldwide (Polanczyk et al. 2007). While there is variability in the rate of diagnosis across countries, much of this variability can be accounted for by differences in criteria: "Our findings suggest that geographic location plays a limited role in the reasons for the large variability of

ADHD/HD prevalence estimates worldwide. Instead, this variability seems to be explained primarily by the methodological characteristics of studies" (Polanczyk et al. 2007, 942). Thus, the differential prevalence of the disorder cannot simply be explained by cultural factors (see also Davidovitch et al. 2017).

It is also highly heritable: it is estimated that around 80 percent of the population variance can be accounted for through genetic differences (Kooij et al. 2019). This is based on studies comparing rates of ADHD across members of a family, in identical and fraternal twins, and for adopted versus biological children. For this reason, researchers have long sought a genetic cause of ADHD. Candidates include those genes related to dopamine, a neurotransmitter that plays an important role in mental control (Cools 2016). While the dopamine transporter gene is implicated in some studies, a meta-analysis finds more promising evidence for dopamine receptor genes: "There is a statistically significant association between ADHD and dopamine system genes, especially *DRD4* and *DRD5*. These findings strongly implicate the involvement of brain dopamine systems in the pathogenesis of ADHD" (Li et al. 2006, 2276).

While dopamine clearly plays a role in ADHD, this role is complex since dopamine enables different functions depending on the level of dopamine, the receptor type, and the neural region. One way of thinking about dopamine is that it tracks and determines resource allocation, with mental control and attention both dependent on cognitive resources (in contrast to, e.g., motor resources; Berke 2018). Certain dopamine receptors (D1 receptors) manage the resource conflict between top-down and bottom-up signals, maintaining attention to the current task, whereas other dopamine receptors (D2 receptors) manage the resource conflict between different top-down signals, determining when to switch to a new task (Bensmann et al. 2020). The activation of these receptors depends on the amount of dopamine, with high levels of dopamine required to activate D1 receptors and lower levels required to activate D2 receptors (Stahl 2017). The determination of when to stay with a task or to switch to a new task is thus sensitive to the level of dopamine, and "the optimum amount of dopamine in prefrontal cortex is an intermediate amount; too much or too little dopamine results in poorer performance on cognitive tasks dependent on prefrontal cortex" (Diamond 2007, i165). For this reason, people react differently to drugs that increase dopamine, with mental control in some benefited by additional dopamine (i.e. those with high impulsivity) and harmed in others (i.e. those with low impulsivity; Cools 2008).

Beyond genetic factors, early childhood experiences are also linked to ADHD. In 1902 Still offered one of the earliest descriptions of ADHD in a medical setting, suggesting a link to brain damage: "He noted that the disorder manifested itself in patterns of restless, inattentive, and overaroused behaviors. He suggested that the children had likely experienced brain damage but that the behavior could also arise from hereditary and environmental factors" (Wolraich et al. 2019, 86). Still's description of ADHD was rooted in social stigma, and it would be wrong to suggest that those with ADHD generally have brain damage (see, e.g., Mueller et al. 2012).[30] Yet, other forms of trauma are still considered to play a significant role in ADHD (see, e.g., Szymanski, Sapanski, and Conway 2011). For example, there is a link between ADHD and so-called "adverse childhood experiences" (ACEs) (e.g. poverty, divorce, and violence): "There was a significant association between ACE score, ADHD, and moderate to severe ADHD" (Brown et al. 2017, 349). Due to the persistence across generations of the social conditions associated with ACEs, one might consider ACEs, and perhaps even trauma, to be an additional cause of ADHD heritability (Schofield et al. 2018; Dias and Ressler 2014).

5.2 ADHD and Mental Control

Both the neurophysiological underpinnings and cognitive/behavioral impacts of ADHD are heterogenous. A common trend is the reduced ability to filter distractors, a hallmark of selective attention (Mueller et al. 2017). In one study, this susceptibility to distractors was found to continue into adolescence for those with ADHD in contrast to a control group, which tended to be less distractible in adolescence (Slobodin, Cassuto, and Berger 2018). Indeed, adults with ADHD continue to demonstrate both reduced inhibitory control and reduced neural signatures of such control (Woltering et al. 2013). This leads some to conclude that "deficits in inhibitory control might be the core of ADHD" (Slobodin, Cassuto, and Berger 2018, 1340).

Yet, some researchers have debated whether ADHD primarily impacts mental control or motivation (e.g. Dekkers et al. 2017). After all, one might fail to inhibit distractors either because one is unable to do so or because one is not motivated to do so. One reason to suspect issues of motivation comes from the fact that those with ADHD both tend to have lower motivation overall and to perform similarly to controls in the case of high motivation. For example, children with ADHD perform similarly to controls when task demands are high: "When performing easy tasks, ADHD children were much slower and

---

[30] Unfortunately, this social stigma persists today and is stronger in certain cultural settings (see, e.g., Fleischmann and Dabbah 2019). Yet, interviews with children who have been diagnosed with ADHD reveal that they are able to maintain a sense of autonomy and control with respect to the disorder: "They neither fully accept nor fully reject the medical definition of their experience but actively work to redefine the experience to make it meaningful to them" (Brady 2014, 223).

made more errors than healthy adults and children ... When performing difficult discriminations, ADHD children were able to filter out distractors as efficiently as healthy adults and children" (Friedman-Hill et al. 2010, 99). In addition, children with ADHD perform similarly to controls when task incentives are high (Liddle et al. 2011). So this disorder appears to find expression in cases of low motivation.

We can understand these differences in motivation through the dopamine system, linking low motivation to inattention. As one study puts it, "Disruption of the dopamine reward pathway is associated with motivation deficits in ADHD adults, which may contribute to attention deficits" (Volkow et al. 2011, 1148). Specifically, those ADHD patients with fewer D2 and D3 receptors tended to have lower motivation, and low motivation was found to strongly correlate with inattention (Volkow et al. 2011). Other studies have found changes in D1 receptors to correspond with inattention for those with ADHD (Misener et al. 2004). So it seems likely that low numbers of dopamine receptors and/or low levels of dopamine can cause both low motivation and inattention in those with ADHD.

We can also understand the link between ADHD and mental control from a wave dynamics perspective, in line with the account provided in subsection 4.2 (see also Section 6). That is, recall that neural firing can be represented in wave form: frequency represents how often the neurons fire, whereas amplitude represents how many neurons fire, or how intensely they fire.[31] "Nesting" occurs when waves or oscillations combine. In Figure 3, a lower frequency, higher amplitude wave is represented by **a** and higher frequency, lower amplitude waves are represented by **b** and **c**, with **d** representing the combination of all three waves. The impact of a on d can be greater than that of b and c, since the amplitudes of b and c are smaller (e.g. at i all three waves are at a low point with c at its maximum amplitude, but the amplitude of a is nonetheless greater, and so its contribution to d is greater). If **b** and **c** are to have an impact on the behavioral outcomes of the organism, they must wait until **a** is at its weakest. This is referred to as "nesting," since the components of **b** and **c** *over time* become nested within the components of **a** in the combined wave. Specifically, the amplitudes of **b** and **c** are ultimately nested within the phase of **a**, such that when the amplitudes of **b** and **c** are high, the phase of **a** is low, and vice versa. This effect has been observed many times in human brains, where it is said that "low-frequency oscillations modulate local cortical

---

[31] For waves, *frequency* is the number of wave cycles per unit of time, *amplitude* is the absolute distance of the wave from equilibrium, and *phase* specifies a specific point within the wave cycle.

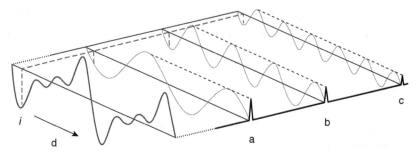

Figure 3 When lower amplitude, higher frequency sine waves (**c**) are combined with higher amplitude, lower frequency sine waves (**a**), the result is a complex wave (**d**). The amplitude of the complex wave (**d**) is the combined amplitude of its component waves (**a**, **b**, **c**). Take the amplitude at *i*: this is the sum of the amplitude at **a**, **b**, and **c** at that moment in time. Since at that point all the amplitudes are in the same direction the overall amplitude is higher than its components. If the amplitudes were in different directions, then the overall amplitude would be smaller than its components.

activity" (Voytek et al. 2010, 1). That is, low-frequency waves, which reflect neural activity from across the brain (i.e. "global" activity), make a difference to ("modulate") high-frequency waves, associated with smaller brain regions (i.e. "local" activity).

Given this background, we might understand mental control as the nesting of high-frequency waves within low-frequency waves. In such an account, the low-frequency waves associated with mental control would make a difference to the high-frequency waves associated with what is being controlled (see Section 6). In this kind of account, we would expect to see changes in low-frequency waves in those with ADHD. There are different levels of control that we might look for here: the control of task over distractors (top-down over bottom-up attention), the control of one task over another, and the control of when to be on- or off-task altogether. I will examine these through two types of low-frequency waves: alpha and "infraslow" waves.

First, the control of top-down over bottom-up attention involves prefrontal cortex. As is mentioned in subsection 3.1, bottom-up attention corresponds with higher frequency waves, such as gamma, whereas top-down attention corresponds with lower frequency waves, such as alpha and beta (see, e.g., Buschman and Miller 2007).[32] ADHD is sometimes linked to lower alpha power in frontal

---

[32] It is standard to divide waves by frequency, with the highest frequency brain waves in the gamma range, followed by beta, alpha, theta, and delta. Researchers differ somewhat on the exact dividing points for these ranges, but one might approximate them as follows: "delta (1–4 Hz),

cortex, as we would expect from this account (see, e.g., Loo and Smalley 2008; Deiber et al. 2020).[33] Moreover, difficulty inhibiting distractors has been correlated with lower alpha power in those with ADHD: "Critically, in ADHD patients only . . . increases in alpha . . . predicted intra-individual reductions in commission errors, indicating task-related alpha power and alpha ERD as significant mediators of inhibitory control" (Deiber et al. 2020, 8). And lower alpha power in frontal cortex has been shown to run in families with ADHD: "Children who had at least one parent with ADHD exhibited significantly lower frontal alpha power during cognitive activation than children who did not have a parent with ADHD" (Loo and Smalley 2008, 108). Thus, alpha power in frontal cortex may correspond with the ability to reduce distractors – such as those represented by bottom-up stimulation – through top-down attention.

Second, competition between tasks likewise involves prefrontal cortex. I discussed above the role of dopamine and specific dopamine receptors in determining whether one should stick with the current task or switch to a new task; in ADHD fewer dopamine receptors and/or reduced dopamine levels contribute to an overall tendency to switch rather than stay (since more dopamine is required to activate the stay receptors). Alpha power has also been implicated in this overall tendency. Specifically, hemispheric differences in alpha power show up in ADHD and in other prefrontal disorders, relative to healthy controls; whereas less alpha power in the left and more alpha power in the right hemisphere tends to correspond with an "approach" tendency ("the impulse to go toward"; Harmon-Jones, Harmon-Jones, and Price 2013, 291), less alpha power in the right and more alpha power in the left hemisphere tends to correspond with an "avoidance" tendency ("increased behavioral inhibition"; Smith et al. 2017, 105). One explanation of this is that the approach tendency corresponds with less alpha power on the left side, leading to less regulation of approach emotions that tend to be left lateralized (e.g. joy and anger), and more alpha power on the right side, leading to more regulation of avoidance emotions that tend to be right lateralized (e.g. fear and anxiety; see, e.g., Elliot 2006, 111).[34] The rightward asymmetry corresponding to an approach tendency has been observed in both children and adults with ADHD (Keune et al. 2015).

---

theta (4–8 Hz), alpha (8–12 Hz), beta (15–30 Hz), and gamma-band oscillations (>30 Hz)" (Amo et al. 2017, 1).

[33] Yet, more research is needed on this topic given the different findings on power bands and ADHD, and whether ADHD subtypes correspond with different alpha-power subtypes (Deiber et al. 2020).

[34] An alternative explanation is that "individuals with greater alpha power in the right frontal hemisphere may be less able to regulate (i.e. inhibit) strong affective states" (Sikka et al. 2019, 4775).

Further, this frontal asymmetry is predictive of the failure to inhibit distractors in those with ADHD (Ellis et al. 2017).

Finally, the determination of whether to be on- or off-task can be linked to wave activity of a different sort: infraslow waves (0.01– 0.1 Hz; Monto et al. 2008). As discussed in subsection 4.2, mind wandering can be understood as unguided thought that occurs when dlPFC activity is low, whether due to exhaustion or simply periodic waning, and is typically brought about due to spontaneous neural activity that is able to capture internal attention, which is managed by vmPFC. Whereas dlPFC is part of the so-called task-positive network (TPN) that governs ongoing attention-demanding tasks, vmPFC is part of the "default-mode" network that is active when not engaged in a task; these networks tend to alternate for dominance (Majeed et al. 2011). This alternation is captured by what is called a "quasi-periodic pattern": "The pattern lasts approximately 20 s in humans. It involves an initial increase in BOLD signal in the DMN accompanied by a decrease in BOLD signal in the TPN. This is followed by a subsequent decrease in BOLD signal in the DMN alongside an increase in BOLD signal in the TPN" (Abbas, Bassil, and Keilholz 2019, 197).[35] While this pattern is also present in those with ADHD, it is weaker: "Individuals with ADHD showed weaker overall connectivity with the DMN and TPN and weaker anti-correlation across the DMN and TPN" (Abbas, Bassil, and Keilholz 2019, 197).[36]

The alternation between TPN and DMN appears to be related to neurochemical modulation. That is, the alternation can be modified through the locus coeruleus, which manages noradrenaline (Abbas, Nezafati, Thomas, and Keilholz 2018). The ability of locus coeruleus (LC) to distribute noradrenaline to PFC wanes over time ("extended LC firing at 10 Hz for 10 min resulted in decreased NA [noradrenaline] levels in the PFC"), and the alternation between TPN and DMN may be in service of preserving this resource (Van Dort 2016, 143). How is this related to ADHD? Relevant to our purposes, "the LC noradrenaline system plays an important part in mediating shifts in attention and in promoting optimal behavioural performance," in part due to its engagement with the dopamine system (Sara 2009, 220). Thus, noradrenaline may not itself be affected in those with ADHD but may typically have the role of increasing the impact of both TPN and DMN. In that case, the reason that those with ADHD have less anticorrelation between TPN and DMN may be

---

[35] BOLD is the primary brain response measured by fMRI, or functional magnetic resonance imaging, and stands for "blood-oxygen level dependent."

[36] Anticorrelation is just negative correlation – an increase in one is associated with a decrease in the other.

simply that these networks are weaker in those with ADHD, due in part to differences in the dopamine system.

5.3 The Phenomenon of Hyperfocus

As mentioned at the start of this section, the differences in mental function associated with ADHD may have advantages in certain situations. Namely, those with ADHD frequently report engaging in the phenomenon of "hyperfocus": "Hyperfocus, broadly and anecdotally speaking, is a phenomenon that reflects one's complete absorption in a task, to a point where a person appears to completely ignore or 'tune out' everything else" (Ashinoff and Abu-Akel 2019, 1). I frequently experience something like hyperfocus while coding, sometimes sitting in one spot for many hours engrossed in the task. Hyperfocus can occur in anyone but is more common in those with ADHD: "Patients with ADHD experience hyperfocus more often than healthy, neurotypical controls both in general and across a range of specific settings (in school, during hobbies, during 'screen time', and in the 'real world')" (Ashinoff and Abu-Akel 2019, 10). What is more, those with more significant ADHD symptoms tend to have more intense and more frequent hyperfocus experiences (Hupfeld, Abagis, and Shah 2019).

One thing to note about hyperfocus is that whether it is advantageous will depend on the situation. That is, if one is trying to finish a coding project in a short time frame then hyperfocus can be an advantage, since one is less likely to be distracted by other projects or interests; however, those other projects and interests may include eating food, drinking water, sleeping, exercising, or other activities conducive to health. Thus, a dispositional trait of being more likely to engage in hyperfocus may not be an advantage for one's overall health, while it may be an advantage for completing certain projects or engaging in certain activities. For example, those with ADHD have been found to use recent digital technologies, such as social media, to a more significant degree than controls, both overall and at night, when others might prioritize rest (Guntuku et al. 2019).[37]

Another thing to note about hyperfocus is that it appears to be paradoxical: those with an attention disorder appear to have a greater ability to focus, at least in certain circumstances. This is especially noteworthy given the previous discussion on dopamine receptors and the supposed consequence of decreased ability for those with ADHD to stay on-task. It is not necessarily paradoxical,

---

[37] But this may have to do with impulsivity rather than hyperfocus. In general, "social media language is predictive of ADHD with an out-of-sample accuracy of 78.5%," likely due to differences in impulsivity (Guntuku et al. 2019, 8).

however, if we distinguish focus from attention. In ADHD, the disorder concerns the ability to direct or control one's focus, not focus itself. As I have defined it in my own work, attention is the activity of prioritizing mental processing by a subject, which ideally results in the subject's focus on their preferred mental processing (e.g. Jennings 2020a). But focus can also come about through lower-level selective mechanisms, such as filtering. Thus, the mere fact of focus does not indicate the presence of attention, in my view (see also Section 3). How might one explain hyperfocus, in that case? One possibility is that lowered dopamine levels or decreased sensitivity to dopamine in certain instances prevent task switching by prefrontal cortex. That is, rather than staying on-task due to increased dopamine activating D1 receptors, neither D1 nor D2 receptors are sufficiently activated, allowing the behavior to continue without interruption by dlPFC. This would only work for a task that is intrinsically rewarding, but those are the very sorts of tasks typically associated with hyperfocus. Perhaps counting against this account, however, is the finding that hyperfocus occurs just as much in those who take stimulants that increase dopamine as in those who do not (Özel Kizil et al. 2016). Clearly, further research is required to understand this phenomenon.

This Element has so far covered mental control and its connection to attention in everyday activities such as ping-pong, as well as in meditation, mind wandering, and ADHD. In the next and final section, I will provide an emergent account of mental control. In my view, this account helps us to resolve some philosophical puzzles concerning mental control, including the problem of mental causation and the homunculus fallacy, introduced in Section 1.

6 The Emergence of Control

Many contemporary accounts of mental control implicitly make use of the concept of *emergence*. Recall from Section 2 that mental control is control *of* the mind *by* the mind, with the mind in the first place serving as object and in the second place serving as subject. What is the difference between mind as subject and mind as object? One possibility is that one part of the mind serves as object and another serves as subject. The part of the mind that serves as subject may be constant, as with the concept of a homunculus, or changeable, with no single part of the mind responsible for mental control. In the latter case, one might claim that what unifies the phenomenon of mental control is an apparently emergent property that comes about as a result of the interaction between these parts. Another possibility is that some part of the mind serves as object whereas the mind *as a whole* serves as subject. This idea is likewise based on the concept of emergence, albeit a stronger form.

Emergence refers to a situation in which a group of entities has properties at the level or spatial scale of the group that exceed the properties of the members of that group; in that case the emergent group and its new properties are said to "emerge" from the members of the group. This can be contrasted with reduction. As Thompson puts it, "Discussions of emergence are structured by the classical opposition between reductionism and emergentism" (2007, 417). In reductionism, a group of entities has only those properties held at the level of ultimate reduction. For example, a molecule may have only those properties held at the level of its component atoms, rather than at the level of the molecule. Of course, the level of ultimate reduction is not necessarily the atomic level: it may occur at a smaller spatial scale.[38] In emergentism, on the other hand, a group of atoms may have new properties at other levels, such as at the level of the molecule.

The specific properties that can be held by emergent entities and the precise relationship between the emergent group and its members are live topics of debate. One debate, for example, concerns whether the properties in question exist (ontological or metaphysical emergence) or are merely apparent (epistemological emergence).[39] Whereas epistemological emergence is about our access to the group being different in some way from our access to the members of the group, ontological emergence is about the group itself being different in some way from the members of the group. For our examples at the start, epistemological emergence would describe the case in which mental control only appears to emerge from interactions between various parts of the mind, whereas metaphysical emergence would describe the case in which the mind as a whole has an impact on its parts. Epistemological emergence is taken to be a "weaker" form of emergence, in that it makes fewer metaphysical commitments. It avoids, for example, attributing causal powers to the emergent in question, which avoids the problem of downward or circular causation – namely, if the emergent depends on its components, how can it have causal power over its components?

Emergence is a hot topic both in philosophy and neuroscience, with prominent theorists on executive control commonly formulating emergence-based views. Some of these theories seem to make use of ontological emergence: "Volitional control is what makes working memory special. It is the fundamental function by which our brain wrests control of behavior from the environment and

---

[38] Some have in fact argued against reductionism on the grounds that the ultimate level of reduction is unspecified or unclear.

[39] While metaphysical emergence is often called "strong emergence," and epistemological emergence is often called "weak emergence," there is substantial variation in the use of these terms (i.e. "weak" and "strong").

turns it to our own internal goals ... Volition is, necessarily, a network phenom-enon and thus not well addressed at the single-neuron level" (Miller, Lundqvist, and Bastos 2018, 463; see also Pinotsis and Miller 2022). Others seem to embrace epistemological emergence: "In distributed systems, control and controlled pro-cesses are colocalized within large numbers of dispersed computational agents. Control then is often an emergent consequence of simple rules governing the interaction between agents" (Eisenreich, Akaishi, and Hayden 2017, 1684). In this section I will discuss different types of emergence and how they contribute to the debate on mental control by way of making the case for stronger forms of emergence, in which the emergent mind as subject controls a part of the mind as object.

6.1 Traditional Forms of Emergence

The primary division between forms of emergence is the epistemic/ontological divide mentioned above. Ontological emergence is conceptually and historic-ally prior. In this form of emergence, something new emerges when certain things get together in the right circumstances. An intuitive example is the emergence of a new plant from a seed. One might think of this as *diachronic* emergence, such that a seed and water at one moment in time emerges as a seedling at another. Yet philosophers have long focused on the more challen-ging to establish *synchronic* emergence: the relationship between the seedling and its components at a single moment in time (see Figure 4).[40] Is there a sense in which the seedling emerges from its component parts? Is that emergence in the sense of the existence of something new, beyond those component parts? If so, this would be a case of ontological emergence.

Thompson (2007), mentioned earlier, contrasts ontological emergence with ontological reduction, in which case "the relations between the parts of the system are all determined without remainder by the intrinsic properties of the most basic parts" (217). If we think of the seedling's component parts as its cells, the relations between the cells would be determined without remainder by their intrinsic properties. Of course, certain relations between the cells will depend on external factors, such as the relative location of light sources. To include those factors we may have to expand the system. Once we have expanded the system to include all the relevant factors, such as light, we ask ourselves whether the component parts of that system determine all the relations in the system, or whether there are properties at the level of the system that also have a role. Can all of the changes in the cells of the plant be accounted for by the properties of those cells, the presence of photons, etc., or do we also need to

---

[40] See O'Connor 2020 for historical accounts of both diachronic and synchronic emergentism.

diachronic emergence

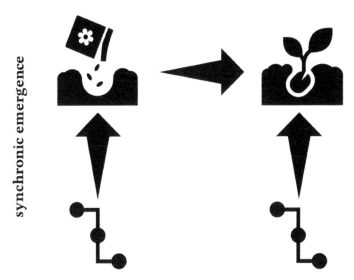

Figure 4 *Diachronic emergence* occurs between moments in time, as when a seedling emerges from a seed, whereas *synchronic emergence* occurs at a moment in time, as when a seed or seedling emerges from its components.

include information about the relationship between the light source and the plant as a whole? In the latter case, we have an instance of ontological emergence.

Ontological emergence has been seen by many philosophers to be a threat to the scientific enterprise; as Bedau puts it, "Strong emergence starts where scientific explanation ends" (2002, 11). Yet, "strong" emergentists were initially inspired by scientific phenomena. Mill, for example, argued that the sorts of interactions that occur in chemistry afford an emergentist perspective; hydrogen and oxygen appear to create something new when they form water, a form of diachronic emergence.[41] Mill called this sort of interaction between chemicals "heteropathic," in contrast with the "homopathic" interactions of, say, forces in physics (O'Connor 2020).[42]

Mill's work on diachronic emergence inspired the tradition of British Emergentism, in which nature is organized into a "hierarchy of levels of organizational complexity of material particles," a form of strong synchronic emergence (McLaughlin 2008, 20). In this tradition, physical interactions might

---

[41] McLaughlin's more scientifically informed example is that of methane and oxygen combining to form carbon dioxide and water (2008).

[42] One might see such heteropathic interactions as bringing about both diachronic and synchronic emergence, but O'Connor sees Mill as having a primarily "dynamical" account of emergence (O'Connor 2020).

be studied through physics, but chemical interactions should be studied through chemistry, and each level has some degree of autonomy. British Emergentism solves the problem of downward causation by introducing "configurational forces," or forces that come about only for particular configurations or structures: "The property of having a certain type of structure will thus endow a special science kind with emergent causal powers" (McLaughlin 2008, 20). Unfortunately, as McLaughlin points out, empirical evidence of the last century has made this solution unattractive.[43]

While certain claims of British Emergentism have come to be seen as disproven or even unscientific, Mill's claims seem to have survived the advancements of the last century: "Does this mean the Emergentists were right about there being emergents? In a word, yes. There are emergent or heteropathic effects, and emergent powers" (McLaughlin 2008, 38). What is different about Mill's claims? For one, Mill focused on diachronic, rather than synchronic, emergence, which has the advantage of avoiding some of the problems of synchronic emergence. Namely, since the emergent entity is brought about by earlier components, its causal power over its current components is not circular, solving the problem of downward causation (see, e.g., O'Connor 2020). Most contemporary emergentists have followed Mill's lead in focusing on diachronic emergence.

Besides focusing on diachronic emergence, Mill's claims may allow for a weaker form of emergence, escaping the problem of downward causation in a different way. Recall that epistemological emergence has to do with knowledge or access: "Epistemological emergentism states that the best understanding of a system is to be found at the level of the structure, behavior, and laws of the whole system" (Thompson 2007, 417). Water might be said to emerge from a certain combination of hydrogen and oxygen at the level of our understanding, while being no more than a combination of hydrogen and oxygen in reality. Again, because it does not concern metaphysics, this is often called "weak" emergence, in contrast to "strong" ontological emergence, although there is substantial variation in the use of these terms.[44] A challenge for weak emergence is explaining why this apparent difference occurs at the level of understanding if it has no basis in the underlying reality.

---

[43] "Quantum mechanical explanations of chemical bonding in terms of the electro-magnetic force, and the advances this led to in molecular biology and genetics render the doctrines of configurational chemical and vital forces enormously implausible" (McLaughlin 2008, 49).

[44] Paoletti (2018), for example, treats epistemic emergence as entirely separable from ontological emergence, which then comes in "weak" and "strong" forms.

6.2 Contemporary Forms of Emergence

Contemporary accounts of emergence tend to fall in between weak and strong emergence. Bedau, for example, makes the case for a somewhat stronger form of weak emergence: "Weak emergent phenomena that would be realized in an indefinite variety of different micro contingencies can instantiate robust macro regularities that can be described and explained only at the macro level" (2002, 182). As he argues, certain macrophenomena can be predicted and explained only through simulation, since they are not computationally reducible. Take, for example, a hurricane: The phenomenon of a hurricane is so complex that meteorologists must simulate its path in order to predict and explain it. We necessarily engage with such phenomena at the macrolevel. Yet, all of the causal power at the macrolevel is constituted by the microlevel: the hurricane's power is constituted by the power of the microparticles that make it up. Nonetheless, Bedau argues that this is more than a merely epistemological emergence due to the fact that the hurricane, for instance, could be made up of different microparticles and have the same path, making it autonomous from those microparticles in some respect.

At the other end of the spectrum from Bedau is Baker (e.g. 1995, 2009). Like Bedau, Baker thinks that constitution allows for macro-objects that could have been constituted by different microcomponents (1995, 9), but she rejects the idea that all the properties of the macro-object necessarily supervene over those of its microconstituents (see subsection 3.2 for more on supervenience). She specifically argues this in the case of so-called "intentional" properties: "A statue is constituted by ... some bunch of molecules, but its property of being a statue does not supervene on the properties of the molecules. The thing is a statue in virtue of its place in the art world" (Baker 1995, 132). That is, she argues that constitution concerns the relations between *objects*, while supervenience concerns the relations between *properties*, and that these should be distinguished. For Baker, the emergence of intentional properties with their own causal powers points to a view in between weak emergence and ontological dualism (which she calls "strong emergence"; Baker 2019).

An important thing to note about Baker is that her view of emergence renounces local supervenience, but not global supervenience. Recall from subsection 6.1 that we might have to expand a system beyond a particular entity to include all of the relevant causal factors. When Baker argues that constitution comes apart from supervenience, she argues that the constitution of a particular entity need not align with the supervenience of all the entity's properties over those of the entity's constituent parts, since that entity may have relations with other entities that determine some of its properties. In that case, local supervenience fails, as with the case of the statue. If one were to expand the supervenience base one might be able to account for all of the relevant properties, but Baker's point is that this would take us far beyond the individual statue, such that the supervenience base would be "too broad to be specified or to be useful in explanation" (Baker 2009, 123).

One way to explain the possibility of an emergent property with causal power that does not supervene over the properties of its local constituent base is through Atmanspacher's "contextual emergence," briefly described at the end of subsection 3.2 (e.g. Atmanspacher 2007). Atmanspacher provides a useful breakdown of the possible relationships between an emergent and its component parts, with contextual emergence falling in between what he calls "weak" and "strong" emergence. According to Atmanspacher, weak emergence is a case in which the component parts are necessary and sufficient for the emergent, whereas strong emergence is a case in which the component parts are neither necessary nor sufficient. Supervenience is an in-between case in which the component parts are sufficient but not necessary. In contrast, contextual emergence is a case in which the component parts are necessary but not sufficient for the emergent. To use Atmanspacher's example here, temperature is contextually emergent since the movement of microparticles is necessary but not sufficient for bringing about temperature. As he argues, temperature also depends on thermodynamic equilibrium between the thermal body in question and other nearby thermal bodies. Only in that case will a specific temperature arise from a specific quantity of motion. This is the "context" of contextual emergence.[45]

The difference between Bedau (2002) and Baker (1995, 2009) is between (relatively) weak diachronic emergence and (relatively) strong synchronic emergence. That is, Bedau argues for the emergence of macrolevel, temporally extended patterns with reducible causal powers, whereas Baker argues for the emergence of relational macrolevel properties with nonreducible powers (at least at the local level). Wilson argues that philosophers should eschew weaker forms of emergence, since the debate in philosophy is primarily about metaphysical issues and "an account based in a bare appeal to the advent of macropatterns fails to provide any substantive basis for resolving the dispute at issue" (2019, 162). She explicitly labels many scientific case studies of emergence as

---

[45] In the natural world, these forms of emergence (supervenience and contextual emergence) may come in degrees (see, e.g., Yoshimi 2012a). Further, they may be complementary, with an emergent determined by some combination of its base and its context – lower base dependence requiring higher context dependence, and vice versa. This would help to explain the phenomenon of metaphysical emergence in naturalistic terms: metaphysical emergence occurs when lower base dependence coincides with higher context dependence.

falling into this category (173). She urges that philosophical discussions on emergence focus on *emergent powers*, which she aligns with function: "If a feature (e.g., pain) is associated with a functional role, then it is associated with certain powers" (169).[46] In her view, if a form of emergence comes with emergent powers then it will be of interest to philosophers, but not otherwise.

Winning and Bechtel likewise see a gulf between scientists and philosophers on this issue but argue that both types of emergence – "pattern emergence" (à la Bedau) and "being emergence" (à la Baker) – have value in these discussions (2019, 137). In their view, pattern emergence can provide a form of control in the right circumstances. This control is not a mere description by an abstracting observer, but something that emerges for a system that itself abstracts. How does a system abstract? Through rate independence, a phenomenon that they say separates biology from physics. Rate independence occurs when a binary signal replaces a continuous one. For example, when you flip a light switch you replace a continuous electrical source with a binary signal; just as an electrician treats the rate dependent and rate independent information about a circuit as both important and complementary, we might treat the rate dependent and rate independent features of nature as both important and complementary. According to Winning and Bechtel, rate independence allows for abstraction, which allows for control, a real feature of biological systems.[47]

In what follows I will make use of both of the above concepts: emergent powers and emergent control. Both seem to me to distinguish the forms of emergence that are of interest to philosophers from merely epistemological forms. And both are useful in constructing an account of mental control.

6.3 A Neuroscientific Account of Emergent Mental Control

How can emergence help to explain how the mind has control over itself? While most accounts of mental control implicitly make use of the concept of emergence, metaphysical specificity is hard to find. In this subsection I will provide a "how-possible" account of mental control that combines many of the above ideas on emergence with recent work in neuroscience.

While we have discussed the meaning of "mental control" – control of the mind by the mind – we do not yet have an understanding of the mind itself. For our purposes, we might think of the mind in terms of interests (à la Bradley) – tendencies to seek out and respond to stimuli in a certain kind of way. We might

---

[46] See also Baysan and Wilson 2017: "Feature F has power C(K,E) just in case an instance of F, in circumstances K, causes (or contributes to causing) an instance of E, and the holding of K alone does not cause (or contribute to causing) instances of E" (63).

[47] This is similar to the account of agency in Mascolo and Kallio (2019), discussed in subsection 3.2.

think of the collection of interests as the emergent mind, and the individual interests as the components or parts of the mind. Mental control could thus be any case in which one's interests are managed by the collection of interests.[48]

I assume in this subsection that our interests have neural correlates. As mentioned in subsection 4.2, neural correlates can include areas of the brain, neurochemicals, and oscillatory frequencies, among other features of the brain. For the sake of discussion, let's separate all of the mind's interests into the rough categories of *fluid*, *formed*, and *fixed*, focusing on their associated brain areas.[49] Some interests are relatively *fluid*: my interest in writing this manuscript, for example, is an interest I maintain on a day-to-day basis. These interests depend on coordinating neural areas, such as prefrontal areas. Other interests are *formed*: my interest in dresses, for example, started relatively early in life and has been subsequently supported by both myself and my environment. We might see formed interests as based in the "reward history" of an organism, as described by Awh, Belopolsky, and Theeuwes (2012) (see subsection 3.1). These interests likely rely on coalitions of neural areas managed by the striatum, rather than prefrontal areas. Finally, some interests are *fixed*, whether by nature or early experience: our interest in fast-moving objects, for example, is both present very early in us and very powerful relative to other interests. We might think of "naturally salient" stimuli, as described in Section 3, as related to our fixed interests. These interests can likely rely on structural features of the mind, such as dedicated neural areas.

We can thus reinterpret our sense of attention and mental control in terms of interests, allowing contrast with epistemological accounts, such as the view that attention just comes down to the competition between interests (e.g. Bradley 1886). Recall that our understanding of attention so far is the prioritization of some mental processes over others, often resulting in the selection of one or more mental processes at the expense of others. We can reinterpret this as the prioritization of some interests over others, often resulting in the selection of one or more interests at the expense of others. The selection of a fluid interest would count as top-down attention, whereas the selection of a fixed interest would count as bottom-up attention.[50]

---

[48] In the language of Frankfurt, one might treat interests as first-order desires, and desires based in the *collection* of those interests as second-order desires (1988).

[49] Thanks to Myrto Mylopoulos for pushing me to better specify "interests" years ago.

[50] Formed interests are more complicated. Take, for example, the famous Jiang et al. (2006) study in which participants attended to subconsciously presented erotic nudes only when the sex of the nude aligned with their sexual orientation. It is unclear whether we would want to call this bottom-up attention on the basis of its subconscious presentation, or top-down attention, since it depends on sexual orientation.

Cases in which a fluid interest wins out over a fixed interest are often associated with mental control. Here is a simple example: while writing this manuscript I might open an internet browser to research an article and find myself confronted with an advertisement for a new dress. My fixed interest in fast-moving things might initially draw my attention to the flickering advertisement, while my formed interest in dresses might hold it. But if my attention is drawn to the advertisement, it will be, at least temporarily, at the expense of my fluid interest in the manuscript. Recall subsection 3.1: the key to mental control is not simply attention but voluntary attention, because by separating voluntary from involuntary attention, we can distinguish control by the mind from control by the world. Once an interest is fixed it can be activated by a corresponding stimulus with ease, requiring little to no effort. A fluid interest, on the other hand, requires effort to be activated and sustained. Thus, if a fixed interest (i.e. in fast-moving things) wins out over a fluid interest (i.e. in the manuscript) then it seems as though the mind has been controlled by the stimulus (i.e. the advertisement for the dress), whereas if a fluid interest wins out over a fixed interest it seems as though the mind is controlling itself by suppressing the activation of the fixed interest.

We can go beyond this standard story with a broader account of mental control based on emergence, such that mental control is any case in which one's interests are managed by the collection of interests. The collection of interests might exert control over individual interests that results in the success of any of the three types of interest: fixed, formed, or fluid. It is easier to see the effect of mental control by the set on individual interests when fluid interests win, because fixed interests can win even without the benefit of mental control. Yet, this does not preclude instances in which fixed interests win from being instances of mental control. Returning to our example, the collection of my interests – including the dress and the manuscript – will balance these interests against one another and adjust their impact, resulting in either continued attention to the research or a switch in attention to the advertisement. If mental control is exerted, that means that the whole has made some difference to the outcome in this balance, reducing the impact of the advertisement. Thus, the manuscript need not win out over the dress for mental control to have occurred – it is just a clearer instance of mental control.

This emergence account is potentially consistent with many different views of emergence, from weak to strong. A weak account would be roughly as follows: "One finds operations everywhere, and nowhere is 'an agent' or his 'action' to be seen as a causal constituent. A mental action is just a particular way of having operations combined in order to let control emerge from their very combination" (Proust 2001, 121). That is, in this account the interests compete with one another directly and when an interest wins at the level of the collection of interests we label this "mental control." Along these lines, Wu (2014) writes, "Attention 'emerges' or is 'realized' in competition when the winner takes all of the spiking resources" (60). In contrast, I argue in favor of a stronger form of emergence – contextual emergence.

I argue for contextual emergence on the basis of neural evidence.[51] To understand the significance of this neural evidence, recall that the rate of neural firing can be represented as waves or oscillations, with different rates divided into bands and labeled with Greek letters; these range from high gamma (more than thirty cycles per second) to low delta (fewer than four cycles per second; see subsections 4.2 and 5.2). Further, the intensity of neural firing can be registered through the amplitude of those waves or oscillations, with more intense or just more neural firing leading to higher amplitudes, and less intense or less neural firing leading to lower amplitudes. Finally, the "phase" of a wave indicates if it is currently in its peak (high point) or trough (low point). An important recent finding from cognitive neuroscience is that bottom-up attention is associated with high-frequency, low-amplitude waves, whereas top-down attention is associated with low-frequency, high-amplitude waves (Buschman and Miller 2007).[52] This difference allows for control by top-down attention over bottom-up attention through nesting (see subsection 5.2), but only when considered in the context of emergence (see, e.g., Szczepanski et al. 2014). That is, the emergence of a wave that combines the elements of relatively high-frequency, low-amplitude oscillations associated with neural activity in one brain area and low-frequency, high-amplitude oscillations associated with neural activity in another brain area is what allows for nesting.

A weak emergentist might claim that this is a mere description of neural activity that does not correspond with any real functionality – high-frequency waves simply *appear* to be nested within low-frequency waves, but this does not occur for any larger purpose. In opposition to this viewpoint are findings that this pattern changes depending on the broader context (hence, "contextual" emergence). In one study, for example, it was found that nesting depends on the type of task: "The preferred low-frequency brain rhythm modulating high gamma amplitude is dependent on the task-specific modality" (Voytek et al.

---

[51] I have elsewhere argued in favor of this contextual-emergence approach to mental control based on the relationship between top-down and bottom-up attention (Jennings 2020a). In sum, the fact that exerting top-down over bottom-up attention comes along with phenomenological (i.e. the feeling of effort), behavioral (i.e. reaction time), and neural evidence (i.e. frequency differences) most consistent with emergent control is a reason to favor this explanation (see Section 3 for more on this evidence).

[52] Frequency and amplitude in the brain have been found to be inversely correlated in numerous studies (see, e.g., Linkenkaer-Hansen et al. 2001).

2010, 6).[53] Another study found that the disruption of nesting depends on the task: "Our results are a first demonstration of how directed interactions affect cross-frequency coupling in downstream areas depending on task demands" (Pascucci, Hervais-Adelman, and Plomp 2018, 3854). While this research paradigm is in its infancy, there is a growing consensus that these patterns have a functional role: "We provide direct evidence that top-down signals can change the phase of relevant oscillatory activity in a perceptually relevant manner" (Veniero et al. 2021, 9).

To summarize, mental control is an emergent phenomenon that depends on the combination of both top-down and bottom-up neural signals in the brain. The combination of these signals leads to a pattern that allows top-down attention to constrain the impact of bottom-up signals, depending on the context. Beyond this account of mental control, we might additionally conclude that the ability to direct our attention in this way leads to *lateral causal power* – causal power of the organism over its environment.

In contrast to lateral causal power is *vertical causal power*. Thompson (2007), for example, offers an analysis of emergent control in terms of "downward causation": "This influence corresponds to the organizational constraint of a system with respect to its components" (427). Gillett (2016), on the other hand, avoids the term "causation" in this instance: "Scientific emergentists can endorse a novel kind of 'downward' determination from 'wholes' to their 'parts'. Overlooked by philosophers, this is a species of non-causal, but also non-compositional, determination between composed and component entities focused upon role-shaping or role-constraining, rather than role-filling" (Gillett 2016, 18). Regardless of whether we think of mental control in terms of downward causation or downward determination in this case, I argue that mental control leads to causal power for the organism over its environment: a lateral form of causation. That is, the organism interacts with its environment through the coordinating activity of the emergent mind, without which we would describe these interactions through the organism's components (i.e. "automatic" behavior).[54]

Thus, mental control (of the mind over itself) is what allows for mental causation (of the mind over its body and environment). The former happens across spatiotemporal scales (the macromind controls its microcomponents) whereas the latter happens within them (the macromind causes changes in the

---

[53] Specifically, gamma oscillations are nested within different low-frequency bands depending on the task, indicating that the nesting is not a mere description, as in weak emergence.

[54] I am excluding here the automatic behavior that is sensitive to context, which is arguably an emergent phenomenon.

macrobody). This approach does not face the problem of downward or circular causation, described at the beginning of this section.[55]

Note that the above account of mental control is consistent with a nonlocal, distributed view of the mind. Yet, again, it is distinct from the currently popular view in which mental control (weakly) emerges from local rules. In the contextual-emergence account, local rules are insufficient to explain mental control, since mental control also depends on a context beyond the local base. This can be understood through what Yoshimi (2012b) calls an "open dynamical system": "A classical dynamical system is closed, in the sense that it is not exposed to outside influences. On the other hand, cognitive systems (like most systems in nature) are open, in the sense that they are coupled to complex and changing environments" (8). An open dynamical system can be contrasted with a closed dynamical system that would occur in the case of local supervenience.

The account of mental control offered in this section answers some of the criticisms described in earlier sections: it is nonlocal and distributed, avoiding the homunculus fallacy, and it has a natural basis, allowing us to determine the extent to which it should be considered a natural kind. It further provides a metaphysical foundation for the observation that the mind makes a difference, avoiding the counterintuitive notion that the sense of cognitive effort is an illusion.

7 Philosophical Epilogue

This Element has reviewed and synthesized work on mental control and attention, ultimately offering an account of the role of attention in mental control: mental control occurs when the emergent set of interests has an impact on the relative priority of those interests through attention. It also explored how this might be expressed in the brain: slow-wave oscillations that originate in prefrontal cortex help determine the impact of higher frequency waves through phase-amplitude nesting, allowing for a distributed model of mental control. This model corresponds with the felt phenomenon of having an influence on our experience and behavior through exertions of voluntary attention. While playing ping-pong, we might focus our mind while preparing to serve, suppressing other thoughts. As play continues, that focus will sometimes manage to suppress distracting stimuli while other times we may find ourselves caught by a bright flash or an idea, pulling us enough out of the game to slow our response and miss a stroke. All of this takes place, I suggest, through wave dynamics in

---

[55] Nearby views beyond those of Thompson and Gillett include Hasker's work on an emergent self whose causal power derives from attention (2001) and Jordan and Ghin's work on consciousness as contextually emergent (2006).

the brain, supported by electrical activity in individual neurons, neurochemical activity across neurons, and other factors (cell metabolism, blood flow, etc.) that likely complicate this simplified picture. As I have shown, this naturalized account of mental control can help us solve puzzles that have plagued other accounts, such as the homunculus fallacy and the problem of mental causation. It can help us to make sense of other, nearby phenomena such as mind wandering, as well as disorders of control, such as ADHD. So I think this approach has its advantages, even while it leaves significant philosophical and other work on the table.

One such important issue is to specify and taxonomize the types of resources that are at play in mental control and attention. Some resources seem unlikely to be manipulated by the processes described here, such as neural real estate, while others are clear candidates, such as signal-to-noise ratio. Other candidates that seem to play a role are cellular metabolism and neurochemical distribution, but it is unclear how they might be manipulated in the service of mental control and attention. Beyond the brain, the constraints of the body and environment are an essential part of this story, the "context" of contextual emergence. Yet how exactly these constraints are used in the service of mental control is still unclear. A better understanding of these resources and their relationships is a crucial next step in applying and extending this framework.

Another place in which philosophical work would be useful is in further specifying and clarifying the possible relations involved in emergence. The literature on emergence can be overwhelming due, in part, to a lack of shared language. Clarity on the concepts and terms, perhaps even to the level of formalization (as provided by, e.g., Yoshimi 2012a and 2012b), would assist us in comparing accounts. I have tried to collate some of the useful work here – on supervenience versus contextual emergence and on control (Gillett's downward determination) versus causation (emergent powers) – but the project is incomplete without a better understanding of the role of living systems in emergence. Some good work is out there, gestured at here through reference to Winning and Bechtel (2019) and Thompson (2007), but more deeply connecting it to the possibility of mental control would be a significant boon to this research topic.

One problem left unresolved in this Element is Wegner and Schneider's (1989) white bear study; at least in some cases, the attempt to exert mental control leads one to be less effective overall at a task than if one had refrained from mental control. While one might be tempted to pin this on the specific nature of the white bear task, the effect has shown up in other tasks: participants have been found to eat more chocolate, for example, when trying to refrain from thinking about chocolate (Erskine and Georgiou 2010). Meta-analyses have been able to explain some but not all aspects of this effect (see, e.g., Abramowitz, Tolin, and Street 2001; Hagger et al. 2010; Wang, Hagger, and Chatzisarantis 2020). While, again, this does not demonstrate that mental control is ineffective, it does demonstrate that mental control comes with significant costs. Why this is the case will likely be tied to our understanding of mental resources, but especially the resources associated with the exertion of willpower. Understanding just how the exertion of willpower and synchronic mental control differs from strategic, diachronic control will require further philosophical and scientific study.

Future directions for this research might also involve application into other domains, such as the impact of recent digital technologies on attention and mental control. A growing consensus is that recent digital technologies have short-term and perhaps long-term impacts on attention (see, e.g., Jennings and Tabatabaeian, forthcoming). Given the role of attention in allowing for mental control, this is seen by many as a threat to autonomy, whereas others are more equivocal (see, e.g., Bermúdez 2017; Cecutti, Chemero, and Lee 2021). This is a fast-growing field and considerable work is needed from multiple disciplines to tackle these questions.

Finally, one way to support the ideas presented in Section 6 would be through elaboration in the language of network science. This would both better enable experimental application of these ideas and extension to other scales, such as the social scale. Is there a sense in which social groups have control of the sort described here? Without a clearer understanding of the mechanisms at play it is difficult to answer such questions.

Thus, while significant work remains on the topic of mental control, this Element provides a starting point. May you dream of marshmallows, ping-pong, and white bears until you find your own inspiration on this common project.

References

Abbas, A., Bassil, Y., & Keilholz, S. (2019). Quasi-periodic patterns of brain activity in individuals with attention-deficit/hyperactivity disorder. *NeuroImage: Clinical*, *21*, 101653.

Abbas, A., Nezafati, M., Thomas, I., & Keilholz, S. (2018). Quasiperiodic patterns in BOLD fMRI reflect neuromodulatory input. In *International Society for Magnetic Resonance in Medicine 26th Annual Meeting. Abstract* (Abstract 8422). https://cds.ismrm.org/protected/18MProceedings/PDFfiles/1118.html.

Abramowitz, J. S., Tolin, D. F., & Street, G. P. (2001). Paradoxical effects of thought suppression: A meta-analysis of controlled studies. *Clinical Psychology Review*, *21*(5), 683–703.

Abrams, R. A., & Weidler, B. J. (2015). Embodied attention. In J. M. Fawcett, E. F. Risko, & A. Kingstone (Eds.), *The Handbook of Attention*, 301–324. MIT Press.

Ainsworth, B., Eddershaw, R., Meron, D., Baldwin, D. S., & Garner, M. (2013). The effect of focused attention and open monitoring meditation on attention network function in healthy volunteers. *Psychiatry Research*, *210*(3), 1226–1231.

Alexander, A. (1910). The paradox of voluntary attention. *Journal of Philosophy, Psychology and Scientific Methods*, *7*(11), 291–298.

Amo, C., De Santiago, L., Barea, R., López-Dorado, A., & Boquete, L. (2017). Analysis of gamma-band activity from human EEG using empirical mode decomposition. *Sensors*, *17*(5), 989. http://doi.org/10.3390/s17050989.

Ampel, B. C., Muraven, M., & McNay, E. C. (2018). Mental work requires physical energy: Self-control is neither exception nor exceptional. *Frontiers in Psychology*, *9*. https://doi.org/10.3389/fpsyg.2018.01005.

Arango-Muñoz, S., & Bermúdez, J. P. (2018). Remembering as a mental action. In K. Michaelian, D. Debus, & D. Perrin (Eds.), *New Directions in the Philosophy of Memory*, 75–96. Routledge.

Ashinoff, B. K., & Abu-Akel, A. (2019). Hyperfocus: The forgotten frontier of attention. *Psychological Research*, *85*(1), 1–19.

Atmanspacher, H. (2007). Contextual emergence from physics to cognitive neuroscience. *Journal of Consciousness Studies*, *14*(1–2), 18–36.

Awh, E., Belopolsky, A. V., & Theeuwes, J. (2012). Top-down versus bottom-up attentional control: A failed theoretical dichotomy. *Trends in Cognitive Sciences*, *16*(8), 437–443.

Axelrod, V., Rees, G., Lavidor, M., & Bar, M. (2015). Increasing propensity to mind-wander with transcranial direct current stimulation. *Proceedings of the National Academy of Sciences, 112*(11), 3314–3319.

Baddeley, A. (1996). Exploring the central executive. *Quarterly Journal of Experimental Psychology Section A, 49*(1), 5–28.

Baddeley, A. (1998). The central executive: A concept and some misconceptions. *Journal of the International Neuropsychological Society, 4*(5), 523–526.

Baddeley, A. D., & Hitch, G. (1974). Working memory. In G. A. Bower (Ed.), *Recent Advances in Learning and Motivation* (Vol. 8), 47–89. Academic Press.

Baker, L. R. (1995). *Explaining Attitudes: A Practical Approach to the Mind.* Cambridge University Press.

Baker, L. R. (2009). Nonreductive materialism. In B. McLaughlin and A. Beckermann (Ed.), *The Oxford Handbook of Philosophy of Mind,* 109–120. Oxford University Press.

Baker, L. R. (2019). Intentionality and Emergence. In S. Gibb, R. F. Hendry, & T. Lancaster (Eds.), *The Routledge Handbook of Emergence,* 195–205. Routledge.

Balota, D. A., & Marsh, E. J. (Eds.) (2004). *Cognitive Psychology: Key Readings.* Psychology Press.

Barkley, R. A. (1997). *ADHD and the Nature of Self-Control.* Guilford Press.

Baysan, U., & Wilson, J. (2017). Must strong emergence collapse? *Philosophica 91,* 49–104.

Bedau, M. (2002). Downward causation and the autonomy of weak emergence. *Principia: An International Journal of Epistemology, 6*(1), 5–50.

Bench, C., Frith, C. D., Grasby, P. M., et al. (1993). Investigations of the functional anatomy of attention using the Stroop test. *Neuropsychologia, 31*(9), 907–922.

Benjamin, D. J., Laibson, D., Mischel, W., et al. (2020). Predicting mid-life capital formation with pre-school delay of gratification and life-course measures of self-regulation. *Journal of Economic Behavior & Organization, 179,* 743–756.

Bennett, K. (2003). Why the exclusion problem seems intractable, and how, just maybe, to tract it. *Noûs, 37*(3), 471–497.

Bensmann, W., Zink, N., Arning, L., Beste, C., & Stock, A. K. (2020). Dopamine D1, but not D2, signaling protects mental representations from distracting bottom-up influences. *NeuroImage, 204,* 116243. https://doi.org/10.1016/j.neuroimage.2019.116243.

Berke, J. D. (2018). What does dopamine mean? *Nature Neuroscience, 21*(6), 787–793.

Bermúdez, J. P. (2017). Social media and self-control: The vices and virtues of attention. In C. G. Prado (Ed.), *Social Media and Your Brain: Web-Based Communication Is Changing How We Think and Express Ourselves*, 57–74. Praeger.

Bermúdez, J. P. (2021). The skill of self-control. *Synthese*, *199*, 6251–6273.

Bertossi, E., & Ciaramelli, E. (2016). Ventromedial prefrontal damage reduces mind-wandering and biases its temporal focus. *Social Cognitive and Affective Neuroscience*, *11*(11), 1783–1791.

Boayue, N. M., Csifcsák, G., Aslaksen, P., et al. (2020). Increasing propensity to mind-wander by transcranial direct current stimulation? A registered report. *European Journal of Neuroscience*, *51*(3), 755–780.

Bradley, F. H. (1886). Is there any special activity of attention? *Mind*, *11*(43), 305–323.

Brady, G. (2014). Children and ADHD: Seeking control within the constraints of diagnosis. *Children & Society*, *28*(3), 218–230.

Breslow, R., Kocsis, J., & Belkin, B. (1980). Memory deficits in depression: Evidence utilizing the Wechsler Memory Scale. *Perceptual and Motor Skills*, *51*(2), 541–542.

Broersen, L. M., & Uylings, H. B. M. (1999). Visual attention task performance in Wistar and Lister hooded rats: Response inhibition deficits after medial prefrontal cortex lesions. *Neuroscience*, *94*(1), 47–57.

Brown, N. M., Brown, S. N., Briggs, R. D., et al. (2017). Associations between adverse childhood experiences and ADHD diagnosis and severity. *Academic Pediatrics*, *17*(4), 349–355.

Buehler, D. (2018). The central executive system. *Synthese*, *195*(5), 1969–1991.

Buehler, D. (2019). Flexible occurrent control. *Philosophical Studies*, *176*(8), 2119–2137.

Buschman, T. J., & Miller, E. K. (2007). Top-down versus bottom-up control of attention in the prefrontal and posterior parietal cortices. *Science*, *315*(5820), 1860–1862.

Campbell, J. (2010). Control variables and mental causation. *Proceedings of the Aristotelian Society*, *110*(1pt.1), 15–30.

Cattell, J. M. (1886). The time taken up by cerebral operations. *Mind*, *11*(42), 220–242.

Cecutti, L., Chemero, A., & Lee, S. W. (2021). Technology may change cognition without necessarily harming it. *Nature Human Behaviour*, *5*(8), 973–975.

Chaieb, L., Antal, A., Derner, M., Leszczyński, M., & Fell, J. (2019). New perspectives for the modulation of mind-wandering using transcranial electric brain stimulation. *Neuroscience*, *409*, 69–80.

Chau, B. K., Keuper, K., Lo, M., et al. (2018). Meditation-induced neuroplastic changes of the prefrontal network are associated with reduced valence perception in older people. *Brain and Neuroscience Advances, 2*, 2398212818771822.

Christensen, W., Sutton, J., & McIlwain, D. J. (2016). Cognition in skilled action: Meshed control and the varieties of skill experience. *Mind & Language, 31*(1), 37–66.

Christoff, K., Irving, Z. C., Fox, K. C., Spreng, R. N., & Andrews-Hanna, J. R. (2016). Mind-wandering as spontaneous thought: A dynamic framework. *Nature Reviews Neuroscience, 17*(11), 718–731.

Chun, M. M., Golomb, J. D., & Turk-Browne, N. B. (2011). A taxonomy of external and internal attention. *Annual Review of Psychology, 62*, 73–101.

Ciaramelli, E., & Treves, A. (2019). A mind free to wander: Neural and computational constraints on spontaneous thought. *Frontiers in Psychology, 10*. https://doi.org/10.3389/fpsyg.2019.00039.

Clayton, M. S., Yeung, N., & Kadosh, R. C. (2015). The roles of cortical oscillations in sustained attention. *Trends in Cognitive Sciences, 19*(4), 188–195.

Cools, R. (2008). Role of dopamine in the motivational and cognitive control of behavior. *Neuroscientist, 14*(4), 381–395.

Cools, R. (2016). The costs and benefits of brain dopamine for cognitive control. *Wiley Interdisciplinary Reviews: Cognitive Science, 7*(5), 317–329.

Csifcsák, G., Boayue, N. M., Aslaksen, P. M., et al. (2019). Commentary: Transcranial stimulation of the frontal lobes increases propensity of mind-wandering without changing meta-awareness. *Frontiers in Psychology, 10*, 130.

Davidovitch, M., Koren, G., Fund, N., Shrem, M., & Porath, A. (2017). Challenges in defining the rates of ADHD diagnosis and treatment: Trends over the last decade. *BMC Pediatrics, 17*(1), 1–9.

Dayer, A., & Jennings, C. D. (2021). Attention in skilled behavior: An argument for pluralism. *Review of Philosophy and Psychology, 12*(3), 615–638.

Deiber, M. P., Hasler, R., Colin, J., et al. (2020). Linking alpha oscillations, attention and inhibitory control in adult ADHD with EEG neurofeedback. *NeuroImage: Clinical, 25*, 102145. https://doi.org/10.1016/j.nicl.2019 .102145.

Dekkers, T. J., van Rentergem, J. A. A., Koole, A., et al. (2017). Time-on-task effects in children with and without ADHD: Depletion of executive resources or depletion of motivation? *European Child & Adolescent Psychiatry, 26* (12), 1471–1481.

Delvenne, J. F., & Holt, J. L. (2012). Splitting attention across the two visual fields in visual short-term memory. *Cognition, 122*(2), 258–263.

Derrfuss, J., Brass, M., Neumann, J., & von Cramon, D. Y. (2005). Involvement of the inferior frontal junction in cognitive control: Meta-analyses of switching and Stroop studies. *Human Brain Mapping*, *25*(1), 22–34.

Diamond, A. (2007). Consequences of variations in genes that affect dopamine in prefrontal cortex. *Cerebral cortex*, *17*(suppl 1), i161–i170.

Diamond, A. (2013). Executive functions. *Annual Review of Psychology*, *64*, 135–168.

Dias, B. G., & Ressler, K. J. (2014). Parental olfactory experience influences behavior and neural structure in subsequent generations. *Nature Neuroscience*, *17*(1), 89–96.

Domenech, P., Rheims, S., & Koechlin, E. (2020). Neural mechanisms resolving exploitation-exploration dilemmas in the medial prefrontal cortex. *Science*, *369*(6507). https://doi.org/10.1126/science.abb0184.

Du, Y., Krakauer, J. W., & Haith, A. M. (2022). The relationship between habits and motor skills in humans. *Trends in Cognitive Sciences*, *26*(5), 371–387.

Duckworth, A. L., Tsukayama, E., & Kirby, T. A. (2013). Is it really self-control? Examining the predictive power of the delay of gratification task. *Personality and Social Psychology Bulletin*, *39*(7), 843–855.

Eisenreich, B. R., Akaishi, R., & Hayden, B. Y. (2017). Control without controllers: Toward a distributed neuroscience of executive control. *Journal of Cognitive Neuroscience*, *29*(10), 1684–1698.

Elliot, A. J. (2006). The hierarchical model of approach-avoidance motivation. *Motivation and Emotion*, *30*(2), 111–116.

Ellis, A. J., Kinzel, C., Salgari, G. C., & Loo, S. K. (2017). Frontal alpha asymmetry predicts inhibitory processing in youth with attention deficit/hyperactivity disorder. *Neuropsychologia*, *102*, 45–51.

Erskine, J. A., & Georgiou, G. J. (2010). Effects of thought suppression on eating behaviour in restrained and non-restrained eaters. *Appetite*, *54*(3), 499–503.

Fiebelkorn, I. C., Pinsk, M. A., & Kastner, S. (2018). A dynamic interplay within the frontoparietal network underlies rhythmic spatial attention. *Neuron*, *99*(4), 842–853.

Fiebich, A., & Michael, J. (2015). Mental actions and mental agency. *Review of Philosophy and Psychology*, *6*(4), 683–693.

Fleischmann, A., & Dabbah, S. (2019). Negev Bedouin teachers' attitudes toward ADHD and its pharmacological treatment. *Qualitative Health Research*, *29*(3), 418–430.

Fox, K. C., Zakarauskas, P., Dixon, M., Ellamil, M., Thompson, E., & Christoff, K. (2012). Meditation experience predicts introspective accuracy. *PLoS ONE*, *7*(9), e45370. https://doi.org/10.1371/journal.pone.0045370.

Frankfurt, H. G. (1988). Freedom of the will and the concept of a person. In M. F. Goodman (Ed.), *What Is a Person?*, 127–144. Humana Press.

Fridland, E. (2014). They've lost control: Reflections on skill. *Synthese, 191*(12), 2729–2750.

Friedman-Hill, S. R., Wagman, M. R., Gex, S. E., Pine, D. S., Leibenluft, E., & Ungerleider, L. G. (2010). What does distractibility in ADHD reveal about mechanisms for top-down attentional control? *Cognition, 115*(1), 93–103.

Ganeri, J. (2017). *Attention, Not Self.* Oxford University Press.

Garrison, K. A., Scheinost, D., Worhunsky, P. D., et al. (2013). Real-time fMRI links subjective experience with brain activity during focused attention. *NeuroImage, 81*, 110–118.

Gillett, C. (2016). *Reduction and Emergence in Science and Philosophy.* Cambridge University Press.

Guntuku, S. C., Ramsay, J. R., Merchant, R. M., & Ungar, L. H. (2019). Language of ADHD in adults on social media. *Journal of Attention Disorders, 23*(12), 1475–1485.

Grubb, M. A., White, A. L., Heeger, D. J., & Carrasco, M. (2015). Interactions between voluntary and involuntary attention modulate the quality and temporal dynamics of visual processing. *Psychonomic Bulletin & Review, 22*(2), 437–444.

Hagger, M. S., Wood, C., Stiff, C., & Chatzisarantis, N. L. (2010). Ego depletion and the strength model of self-control: A meta-analysis. *Psychological Bulletin, 136*(4), 495–525.

Harmon-Jones, E., Harmon-Jones, C., & Price, T. F. (2013). What is approach motivation? *Emotion Review, 5*(3), 291–295.

Harris, W. T. (1881). Analysis and commentary. *Journal of Speculative Philosophy, 15*(1), 52–62.

Hasker, W. (2001). *The Emergent Self.* Cornell University Press.

Herdova, M. (2017). Self-control and mechanisms of behavior: Why self-control is not a natural mental kind. *Philosophical Psychology, 30*(6), 731–762.

Hohwy, J. (2004). The experience of mental causation. *Behavior and Philosophy, 32*(2), 377–400.

Holton, R., & Shute, S. (2007). Self-control in the modern provocation defence. *Oxford Journal of Legal Studies, 27*(1), 49–73.

Hupfeld, K. E., Abagis, T. R., & Shah, P. (2019). Living "in the zone": Hyperfocus in adult ADHD. *ADHD Attention Deficit and Hyperactivity Disorders, 11*(2), 191–208.

Irving, Z. C. (2016). Mind-wandering is unguided attention: Accounting for the "purposeful" wanderer. *Philosophical Studies, 173*(2), 547–571.

Irving, Z. C., & Glasser, A. (2020). Mind-wandering: A philosophical guide. *Philosophy Compass*, *15*(1), e12644. https://doi.org/10.1111/phc3.12644.

James, W. (1890). *The Principles of Psychology: In Two Volumes* (Vol. 1). Macmillan and Company.

Jennings, C. D. (2012). The subject of attention. *Synthese*, *189*(3), 535–554.

Jennings, C. D. (2020a). *The Attending Mind*. Cambridge University Press.

Jennings, C. D. (2020b). Practical realism about the self. In L. R. G. Oliveira and K. Corcoran (Eds.), *Common Sense Metaphysics: Essays in Honor of Lynne Rudder Baker*, 39–53. Taylor & Francis.

Jennings, C. D. and Tabatabaeian, S. (forthcoming). Attention, technology, and creativity. In D. G. Burnett & J. E. H. Smith (Eds.), *Scenes of Attention: An Interdisciplinary Inquiry*. Columbia University Press.

Jiang, Y., Costello, P., Fang, F., Huang, M., & He, S. (2006). A gender- and sexual orientation-dependent spatial attentional effect of invisible images. *Proceedings of the National Academy of Sciences*, *103*(45), 17048–17052.

Jonides, J. (1981). Voluntary versus automatic control over the mind's eye's movement. In J. Long & A. D. Baddeley (Eds.), *Attention and Performance IX*, 187–203. Erlbaum.

Jordan, J. S., & Ghin, M. (2006). Consciousness as a contextually emergent property of self-sustaining systems. *Mind and Matter*, *4*(1), 45–68.

Kahn, J. B., Ward, R. D., Kahn, L. W., et al. (2012). Medial prefrontal lesions in mice impair sustained attention but spare maintenance of information in working memory. *Learning & Memory*, *19*(11), 513–517.

Kane, M. J., & McVay, J. C. (2012). What mind wandering reveals about executive-control abilities and failures. *Current Directions in Psychological Science*, *21*(5), 348–354.

Kane, M. J., Poole, B. J., Tuholski, S. W., & Engle, R. W. (2006). Working memory capacity and the top-down control of visual search: Exploring the boundaries of "executive attention." *Journal of Experimental Psychology: Learning, Memory, and Cognition*, *32*(4), 749–777.

Kane, R. (1999). Responsibility, luck, and chance: Reflections on free will and indeterminism. *Journal of Philosophy*, *96*(5), 217–240.

Kant, I. (1951). *Critique of Judgment* (J. H. Bernard, Trans.). Hafner Publication.

Kawahara, J., Yanase, K., & Kitazaki, M. (2012). Attentional capture by the onset and offset of motion signals outside the spatial focus of attention. *Journal of Vision*, *12*(12), 10.

Kennett, J., & Wolfendale, J. (2019). Self control and moral security. In D. Shoemaker (Ed.), *Oxford Studies in Agency and Responsibility* (Vol. 6), 33–63. Oxford University Press.

Keune, P. M., Wiedemann, E., Schneidt, A., & Schönenberg, M. (2015). Frontal brain asymmetry in adult attention-deficit/hyperactivity disorder (ADHD): Extending the motivational dysfunction hypothesis. *Clinical Neurophysiology, 126*(4), 711–720.

Kidd, C., Palmeri, H., & Aslin, R. N. (2013). Rational snacking: Young children's decision-making on the marshmallow task is moderated by beliefs about environmental reliability. *Cognition, 126*(1), 109–114.

Kim, J. (2007). *Physicalism, or Something Near Enough*. Princeton University Press.

Kooij, J. J. S., Bijlenga, D., Salerno, L., et al. (2019). Updated European consensus statement on diagnosis and treatment of adult ADHD. *European Psychiatry, 56*(1), 14–34.

Lamm, B., Keller, H., Teiser, J., et al. (2018). Waiting for the second treat: Developing culture-specific modes of self-regulation. *Child Development, 89*(3), e261–e277.

Latham, N. (2016). Meditation and self-control. *Philosophical Studies, 173*(7), 1779–1798.

Laureiro-Martínez, D., Brusoni, S., Canessa, N., & Zollo, M. (2015). Understanding the exploration-exploitation dilemma: An fMRI study of attention control and decision-making performance. *Strategic Management Journal, 36*(3), 319–338.

Lega, C., Ferrante, O., Marini, F., Santandrea, E., Cattaneo, L., & Chelazzi, L. (2019). Probing the neural mechanisms for distractor filtering and their history-contingent modulation by means of TMS. *Journal of Neuroscience, 39*(38), 7591–7603.

Li, D., Sham, P. C., Owen, M. J., & He, L. (2006). Meta-analysis shows significant association between dopamine system genes and attention deficit hyperactivity disorder (ADHD). *Human Molecular Genetics, 15*(14), 2276–2284.

Liddle, E. B., Hollis, C., Batty, M. J., et al. (2011). Task-related default mode network modulation and inhibitory control in ADHD: Effects of motivation and methylphenidate. *Journal of Child Psychology and Psychiatry, 52*(7), 761–771.

Linkenkaer-Hansen, K., Nikouline, V. V., Palva, J. M., & Ilmoniemi, R. J. (2001). Long-range temporal correlations and scaling behavior in human brain oscillations. *Journal of Neuroscience, 21*(4), 1370–1377.

Lippelt, D. P., Hommel, B., & Colzato, L. S. (2014). Focused attention, open monitoring and loving kindness meditation: Effects on attention, conflict monitoring, and creativity – A review. *Frontiers in Psychology, 5*, 1083. https://doi.org/10.3389/fpsyg.2014.01083.

Logie, R. H. (2016). Retiring the central executive. *Quarterly Journal of Experimental Psychology, 69*(10), 2093–2109.

Loheswaran, G., Barr, M. S., Zomorrodi, R., et al. (2018). Alcohol impairs N100 response to dorsolateral prefrontal cortex stimulation. *Scientific Reports, 8*(1), 1–6.

Loo, S. K., & Smalley, S. L. (2008). Preliminary report of familial clustering of EEG measures in ADHD. *American Journal of Medical Genetics Part B: Neuropsychiatric Genetics, 147*(1), 107–109.

Lutz, A., Greischar, L. L., Rawlings, N. B., Ricard, M., & Davidson, R. J. (2004). Long-term meditators self-induce high-amplitude gamma synchrony during mental practice. *Proceedings of the National Academy of Sciences, 101*(46), 16369–16373.

Lutz, A., Slagter, H. A., Dunne, J. D., & Davidson, R. J. (2008). Attention regulation and monitoring in meditation. *Trends in Cognitive Sciences, 12*(4), 163–169.

MacLeod, C. M., & MacDonald, P. A. (2000). Interdimensional interference in the Stroop effect: Uncovering the cognitive and neural anatomy of attention. *Trends in Cognitive Sciences, 4*(10), 383–391.

Majeed, W., Magnuson, M., Hasenkamp, W., et al. (2011). Spatiotemporal dynamics of low frequency BOLD fluctuations in rats and humans. *NeuroImage, 54*(2), 1140–1150.

Mangun, G. R. (1995). Neural mechanisms of visual selective attention. *Psychophysiology, 32*(1), 4–18.

Mann, T., & Ward, A. (2007). Attention, self-control, and health behaviors. *Current Directions in Psychological Science, 16*(5), 280–283.

Mariani, A. P. (1984). Bipolar cells in monkey retina selective for the cones likely to be blue-sensitive. *Nature, 308*(5955), 184–186.

Mascolo, M. F., & Kallio, E. (2019). Beyond free will: The embodied emergence of conscious agency. *Philosophical Psychology, 32*(4), 437–462.

McClelland, J. L., Botvinick, M. M., Noelle, D. C., et al. (2010). Letting structure emerge: Connectionist and dynamical systems approaches to cognition. *Trends in Cognitive Sciences, 14*(8), 348–356.

McCormick, C., Rosenthal, C. R., Miller, T. D., & Maguire, E. A. (2018). Mind-wandering in people with hippocampal damage. *Journal of Neuroscience, 38*(11), 2745–2754.

McLaughlin, B. (2008). The rise and fall of British Emergentism. In M. A. Bedau and P. Humphreys (Eds.), *Emergence: Contemporary Readings in Philosophy and Science*, 20–59. MIT Press.

McLaughlin, B., & K. Bennett (2021). Supervenience. In E. N. Zalta (Ed.), *The Stanford Encyclopedia of Philosophy*. https://plato.stanford.edu/archives/sum2021/entries/supervenience/.

McVay, J. C., & Kane, M. J. (2010). Does mind wandering reflect executive function or executive failure? Comment on Smallwood and Schooler (2006) and Watkins (2008). *Psychological Bulletin, 136*(2), 188–197.

McVay, J. C., Kane, M. J., & Kwapil, T. R. (2009). Tracking the train of thought from the laboratory into everyday life: An experience-sampling study of mind wandering across controlled and ecological contexts. *Psychonomic Bulletin & Review, 16*(5), 857–863.

Mele, A. R. (2009). *Effective Intentions: The Power of Conscious Will*. Oxford University Press.

Mele, A. R. (2018). Free will, moral responsibility, and scientific epiphenomenalism. *Frontiers in Psychology, 9*, 2536.

Metzinger, T. (2017). The problem of mental action. In T. Metzinger & W. Wiese (Eds.), *Philosophy and Predictive Processing*. MIND Group. https://doi.org/10.15502/9783958573208.

Michaelson, L. E., & Munakata, Y. (2020). Same data set, different conclusions: Preschool delay of gratification predicts later behavioral outcomes in a preregistered study. *Psychological Science, 31*(2), 193–201.

Miller, E. K., Lundqvist, M., & Bastos, A. M. (2018). Working memory 2.0. *Neuron, 100*(2), 463–475.

Miller, E. K., & Wallis, J. D. (2009). Executive function and higher-order cognition: Definition and neural substrates. *Encyclopedia of Neuroscience, 4*, 99–104.

Misener, V. L., Luca, P., Azeke, O., et al. (2004). Linkage of the dopamine receptor D1 gene to attention-deficit/hyperactivity disorder. *Molecular Psychiatry, 9*(5), 500–509.

Mole, C. (2011). *Attention is Cognitive Unison: An Essay in Philosophical Psychology*. Oxford University Press.

Mole, C. (2017). Attention. In E. N. Zalta (Ed.), *The Stanford Encyclopedia of Philosophy*. https://plato.stanford.edu/archives/fall2017/entries/attention/.

Monsell, S., & Driver, J. (2000). Banishing the control homunculus. *Control of Cognitive Processes: Attention and Performance, 18*, 3–32.

Monto, S., Palva, S., Voipio, J., & Palva, J. M. (2008). Very slow EEG fluctuations predict the dynamics of stimulus detection and oscillation amplitudes in humans. *Journal of Neuroscience, 28*(33), 8268–8272.

Moors, A., & Houwer, J. D. (2007). What is automaticity? An analysis of its component features and their interrelations. In J. A. Bargh (Ed.), *Social*

Psychology and the Unconscious: The Automaticity of Higher Mental Processes, 11–50. Psychology Press.

Mueller, A., Hong, D. S., Shepard, S., & Moore, T. (2017). Linking ADHD to the neural circuitry of attention. *Trends in Cognitive Sciences, 21*(6), 474–488.

Mueller, A. K., Fuermaier, A. B., Koerts, J., & Tucha, L. (2012). Stigma in attention deficit hyperactivity disorder. *ADHD Attention Deficit and Hyperactivity Disorders, 4*(3), 101–114.

Muret, D., & Makin, T. R. (2021). The homeostatic homunculus: Rethinking deprivation-triggered reorganisation. *Current Opinion in Neurobiology, 67*, 115–122.

Naccache, L., Dehaene, S., Cohen, L. J., et al. (2005). Effortless control: Executive attention and conscious feeling of mental effort are dissociable. *Neuropsychologia, 43*(9), 1318–1328.

Nahmias, E. (2002). When consciousness matters: A critical review of Daniel Wegner's *The Illusion of Conscious Will*. *Philosophical Psychology, 15*(4), 527–541.

Nejati, V., Majdi, R., Salehinejad, M. A., & Nitsche, M. A. (2021). The role of dorsolateral and ventromedial prefrontal cortex in the processing of emotional dimensions. *Scientific Reports, 11*(1), 1–12.

O'Connor, T. 2020. Emergent properties. In E. N. Zalta (Ed.), *The Stanford Encyclopedia of Philosophy*. https://plato.stanford.edu/archives/fall2020/entries/properties-emergent/.

Özel Kizil, E. T., Öncü, B., Demirbaş, H., et al. (2016). Hyperfocusing as a dimension of adult attention deficit hyperactivity disorder. *Research in Developmental Disabilities, 59*, 351–358.

Pacherie, E., & Mylopoulos, M. (2021). Beyond automaticity: The psychological complexity of skill. *Topoi, 40*(3), 649–662.

Paolini Paoletti, M. (2018). Formulating emergence. *Ratio, 31*, 1–18.

Papineau, D. (2015). Choking and the yips. *Phenomenology and the Cognitive Sciences, 14*(2), 295–308.

Pappas, D. (2006). ADHD rating scale-IV: Checklists, norms, and clinical interpretation. *Journal of Psychoeducational Assessment, 24*(2), 172–178.

Parkin, A. J. (1998). The central executive does not exist. *Journal of the International Neuropsychological Society, 4*(5), 518–522.

Pascucci, D., Hervais-Adelman, A., & Plomp, G. (2018). Gating by induced A–Γ asynchrony in selective attention. *Human Brain Mapping, 39*(10), 3854–3870.

Pinotsis, D. A., & Miller, E. K. (2022). Beyond dimension reduction: Stable electric fields emerge from and allow representational drift. *NeuroImage, 253*, 119058. https://doi.org/10.1016/j.neuroimage.2022.119058.

Plebanek, D. J., & Sloutsky, V. M. (2017). Costs of selective attention: When children notice what adults miss. *Psychological Science, 28*(6), 723–732.

Polanczyk, G., De Lima, M. S., Horta, B. L., Biederman, J., & Rohde, L. A. (2007). The worldwide prevalence of ADHD: A systematic review and metaregression analysis. *American Journal of Psychiatry, 164*(6), 942–948.

Posner, M. I. (1980). Orienting of attention. *Quarterly Journal of Experimental Psychology, 32*(1), 3–25.

Posner, M. I., & Cohen, Y. (1984). Components of visual orienting. *Attention and Performance X: Control of Language Processes, 32*, 531–556.

Posner, M. I., & Gilbert, C. D. (1999). Attention and primary visual cortex. *Proceedings of the National Academy of Sciences, 96*(6), 2585–2587.

Posner, M. I., & Rothbart, M. K. (1998). Attention, self-regulation and consciousness. *Philosophical Transactions of the Royal Society of London Series B: Biological Sciences, 353*(1377), 1915–1927.

Posner, M. I., & Snyder, C. R. R. (2004). Attention and cognitive control. In D. A. Balota & E. J. Marsh (Eds.), *Cognitive Psychology: Key Readings*, 205–223. Psychology Press.

Prinz, J. (2011). Is attention necessary and sufficient for consciousness? In C. Mole, D. Smithies, & W. Wu, (Eds.), *Attention: Philosophical and Psychological Essays*, 174–203. Oxford University Press.

Prinzmetal, W., Zvinyatskovskiy, A., Gutierrez, P., & Dilem, L. (2009). Voluntary and involuntary attention have different consequences: The effect of perceptual difficulty. *Quarterly Journal of Experimental Psychology, 62*(2), 352–369.

Proust, J. (2001). A plea for mental acts. *Synthese, 129*(1), 105–128.

Raichle, M. E. (2015). The brain's default mode network. *Annual Review of Neuroscience, 38*, 433–447.

Reeve, W. V., & Schandler, S. L. (2001). Frontal lobe functioning in adolescents with attention deficit hyperactivity disorder. *Adolescence, 36*(144), 749–765.

Reynolds, J. H., & Desimone, R. (2003). Interacting roles of attention and visual salience in V4. *Neuron, 37*(5), 853–863.

Ribot, T. (1890). *The Psychology of Attention*. Open Court Publishing Company.

Robbins, T. W., & Rogers, R. D. (2000). Functioning of frontostriatal anatomical "loops" in mechanisms of cognitive control. *Control of Cognitive Processes: Attention and Performance, 18*, 3–32.

Robinson, H. (2020). Dualism. In E. N. Zalta (Ed.), *The Stanford Encyclopedia of Philosophy*. https://plato.stanford.edu/archives/fall2020/entries/dualism/.

Rokem, A., Landau, A. N., Garg, D., Prinzmetal, W., & Silver, M. A. (2010). Cholinergic enhancement increases the effects of voluntary attention but does not affect involuntary attention. *Neuropsychopharmacology, 35*(13), 2538–2544.

Rossi, A. F., Pessoa, L., Desimone, R., & Ungerleider, L. G. (2009). The prefrontal cortex and the executive control of attention. *Experimental Brain Research, 192*(3), 489–497.

Sara, S. J. (2009). The locus coeruleus and noradrenergic modulation of cognition. *Nature Reviews Neuroscience, 10*(3), 211–223.

Schack, T., & Frank, C. (2021). Mental representation and the cognitive architecture of skilled action. *Review of Philosophy and Psychology, 12*(3), 527–546.

Schneider, D. (1993). Mental control: Lessons from our past. In D. M. Wegner & J. W. Pennebaker (Eds.), *Handbook of Mental Control*, 13–35. Prentice-Hall, Inc.

Schneider, W., Dumais, S. T., & Shiffrin, R. M. (1982). *Automatic/Control Processing and Attention* (No. HARL-ONR-8104). Illinois Univ. Champaign Human Attention Research Lab. https://apps.dtic.mil/sti/citations/ADA115078.

Schofield, T. J., Donnellan, M. B., Merrick, M. T., Ports, K. A., Klevens, J., & Leeb, R. (2018). Intergenerational continuity in adverse childhood experiences and rural community environments. *American Journal of Public Health, 108*(9), 1148–1152.

Semple, R. J. (2010). Does mindfulness meditation enhance attention? A randomized controlled trial. *Mindfulness, 1*(2), 121–130.

Setyawan, J., Fridman, M., Grebla, R., Harpin, V., Korst, L. M., & Quintero, J. (2018). Variation in presentation, diagnosis, and management of children and adolescents with ADHD across European countries. *Journal of Attention Disorders, 22*(10), 911–923.

Shah, J. Y., Friedman, R. S., & Kruglanski, A. W. (2002). Forgetting all else: On the antecedents and consequences of goal shielding. *Journal of Personality and Social Psychology, 83*, 1261–1280.

Shepherd, J. (2014). The contours of control. *Philosophical Studies, 170*(3), 395–411.

Shepherd, J. (2019). Why does the mind wander? *Neuroscience of Consciousness, 2019*(1), niz014. https://doi.org/10.1093/nc/niz014.

Shoda, Y., Mischel, W., & Peake, P. K. (1990). Predicting adolescent cognitive and self-regulatory competencies from preschool delay of gratification: Identifying diagnostic conditions. *Developmental Psychology, 26*(6), 978–986.

Shomstein, S., Zhang, X., & Dubbelde, D. (2022). Attention and platypuses. *Wiley Interdisciplinary Reviews: Cognitive Science*, e1600. https://doi.org/10.1002/wcs.1600.

Sikka, P., Revonsuo, A., Noreika, V., & Valli, K. (2019). EEG frontal alpha asymmetry and dream affect: Alpha oscillations over the right frontal cortex during REM sleep and presleep wakefulness predict anger in REM sleep dreams. *Journal of Neuroscience*, *39*(24), 4775–4784.

Skinner, B. F. (1984). Behaviorism at fifty. *Behavioral and Brain Sciences*, *7*(4), 615–621.

Slobodin, O., Cassuto, H., & Berger, I. (2018). Age-related changes in distractibility: Developmental trajectory of sustained attention in ADHD. *Journal of Attention Disorders*, *22*(14), 1333–1343.

Smallwood, J., Beach, E., Schooler, J. W., & Handy, T. C. (2008). Going AWOL in the brain: Mind wandering reduces cortical analysis of external events. *Journal of Cognitive Neuroscience*, *20*(3), 458–469.

Smallwood, J., & Schooler, J. W. (2006). The restless mind. *Psychological Bulletin*, *132*(6), 946–958.

Smallwood, J., & Schooler, J. W. (2015). The science of mind wandering: Empirically navigating the stream of consciousness. *Annual Review of Psychology*, *66*, 487–518.

Smith, E. E., Reznik, S. J., Stewart, J. L., & Allen, J. J. (2017). Assessing and conceptualizing frontal EEG asymmetry: An updated primer on recording, processing, analyzing, and interpreting frontal alpha asymmetry. *International Journal of Psychophysiology*, *111*, 98–114.

Somsen, R. J. (2007). The development of attention regulation in the Wisconsin Card Sorting Task. *Developmental Science*, *10*(5), 664–680.

Soutschek, A., & Tobler, P. N. (2020). Causal role of lateral prefrontal cortex in mental effort and fatigue. *Human Brain Mapping*, *41*(16), 4630–4640.

Sripada, C. (2021). The atoms of self-control. *Noûs*, *55*(4), 800–824.

Sripada, C. S. (2018). An exploration/exploitation trade-off between mind wandering and goal-directed thinking. In K. Christoff & K. C. R. Fox (Eds.), *The Oxford Handbook of Spontaneous Thought: Mind-Wandering, Creativity, and Dreaming*, 23–34. Oxford University Press.

Stahl, S. M. (2017). Dazzled by the dominions of dopamine: Clinical roles of D3, D2, and D1 receptors. *CNS Spectrums*, *22*(4), 305–311.

Stoljar, D. (2017). Physicalism. In E. N. Zalta (Ed.), *The Stanford Encyclopedia of Philosophy*. https://plato.stanford.edu/archives/win2017/entries/physicalism/.

Stothart, C., Simons, D. J., Boot, W. R., & Wright, T. J. (2019). What to where: The right attention set for the wrong location. *Perception*, *48*(7), 602–615.

Strömgren, L. S. (1977). The influence of depression on memory. *Acta psychiatrica scandinavica*, *56*(2), 109–128.

Stubenberg, L. (2018). Neutral monism. In E. N. Zalta (Ed.), *The Stanford Encyclopedia of Philosophy*. https://plato.stanford.edu/archives/fall2018/entries/neutral-monism/.

Stuss, D. T., & Alexander, M. P. (2000). Executive functions and the frontal lobes: A conceptual view. *Psychological Research*, *63*(3), 289–298.

Substance Abuse and Mental Health Services Administration. (2016). *DSM-5 Changes: Implications for Child Serious Emotional Disturbance*, Table 7, DSM-IV to DSM-5 attention-deficit/hyperactivity disorder comparison. www.ncbi.nlm.nih.gov/books/NBK519712/table/ch3.t3/.

Szczepanski, S. M., Crone, N. E., Kuperman, R. A., Auguste, K. I., Parvizi, J., & Knight, R. T. (2014). Dynamic changes in phase-amplitude coupling facilitate spatial attention control in fronto-parietal cortex. *PLoS Biology*, *12*(8), e1001936. https://doi.org/10.1371/journal.pbio.1001936.

Szymanski, K., Sapanski, L., & Conway, F. (2011). Trauma and ADHD – Association or diagnostic confusion? A clinical perspective. *Journal of Infant, Child, and Adolescent Psychotherapy*, *10*(1), 51–59.

Tang, Y.-Y., Hölzel, B. K., & Posner, M. I. (2015). The neuroscience of mindfulness meditation. *Nature Reviews Neuroscience*, *16*(4), 213–225.

Tang, Y.-Y., Tang, R., Posner, M. I., & Gross, J. J. (2022). Effortless training of attention and self-control: Mechanisms and applications. *Trends in Cognitive Sciences*, *26*(7), 566–577. www.sciencedirect.com/science/article/pii/S1364661322000900.

Taylor, V. A., Daneault, V., Grant, J., et al. (2013). Impact of meditation training on the default mode network during a restful state. *Social Cognitive and Affective Neuroscience*, *8*(1), 4–14.

Thompson, E. (2007). *Mind in Life*. Harvard University Press.

Tran, D. M. (2020). Commentary: probing the neural mechanisms for distractor filtering and their history-contingent modulation by means of TMS. *Frontiers in Neuroscience*, *14*. https://doi.org/10.3389/fnins.2020.00365.

Uhl, L. L. (1890). *Attention: A Historical Summary of the Discussion concerning the Subject*. Johns Hopkins Press.

Upton, C. L., & Brent, M. (2019). Meditation and the scope of mental action. *Philosophical Psychology*, *32*(1), 52–71.

Valentine, E. R., & Sweet, P. L. (1999). Meditation and attention: A comparison of the effects of concentrative and mindfulness meditation on sustained attention. *Mental Health, Religion & Culture*, *2*(1), 59–70.

Vallacher, R. R. (1993). Mental calibration: Forging a working relationship between mind and action. In D. M. Wegner & J. W. Pennebaker (Eds.), *Handbook of Mental Control*, 443–472. Prentice-Hall, Inc.

Van Dort, C. J. (2016). Locus coeruleus neural fatigue: A potential mechanism for cognitive impairment during sleep deprivation. *Sleep*, *39*(1), 11–12.

Velmans, M. (2002). How could conscious experiences affect brains? *Journal of Consciousness Studies*, *9*(11), 3–29.

Veniero, D., Gross, J., Morand, S., Duecker, F., Sack, A. T., & Thut, G. (2021). Top-down control of visual cortex by the frontal eye fields through oscillatory realignment. *Nature Communications*, *12*(1), 1–13.

Vierkant, T. (2014). Mental muscles and the extended will. *Topoi*, *33*(1), 57–65.

Volkow, N. D., Wang, G. J., Newcorn, J. H., et al. (2011). Motivation deficit in ADHD is associated with dysfunction of the dopamine reward pathway. *Molecular Psychiatry*, *16*(11), 1147–1154.

Voytek, B., Canolty, R. T., Shestyuk, A., Crone, N., Parvizi, J., & Knight, R. T. (2010). Shifts in gamma phase–amplitude coupling frequency from theta to alpha over posterior cortex during visual tasks. *Frontiers in Human Neuroscience*, *4*, 191. https://doi.org/10.3389/fnhum.2010.00191.

Wang, D., Hagger, M. S., & Chatzisarantis, N. L. (2020). Ironic effects of thought suppression: A meta-analysis. *Perspectives on Psychological Science*, *15*(3), 778–793.

Watts, T. W., Duncan, G. J., & Quan, H. (2018). Revisiting the marshmallow test: A conceptual replication investigating links between early delay of gratification and later outcomes. *Psychological Science*, *29*(7), 1159–1177.

Watzl, S. (2011). The nature of attention. *Philosophy Compass*, *6*(11), 842–853.

Watzl, S. (2017). *Structuring Mind: The Nature of Attention and How It Shapes Consciousness*. Oxford University Press.

Wegner, D. M. (1988). Stress and mental control. In S. Fisher & J. Reason (Eds.), *Handbook of Life Stress, Cognition and Health*, 683–697. John Wiley and Sons.

Wegner, D. M. (1994). Ironic processes of mental control. *Psychological Review*, *101*(1), 34–52.

Wegner, D. M. (2004). Précis of *The Illusion of Conscious Will. Behavioral and Brain Sciences*, *27*(5), 649–659.

Wegner, D. M., & Pennebaker, J. W. (1993). Changing our minds: An introduction to mental control. In D. M. Wegner & J. W. Pennebaker (Eds.), *Handbook of Mental Control*, 1–12. Prentice-Hall, Inc.

Wegner, D. M., & Schneider, D. J. (1989). Mental control: The war of the ghosts in the machine. In J. S. Uleman & J. A. Bargh (Eds.), *Unintended Thought*, 287–305. Guilford Press.

Wegner, D. M., Schneider, D. J., Carter, S. R., & White, T. L. (1987). Paradoxical effects of thought suppression. *Journal of Personality and Social Psychology, 53*(1), 5–13.

Wegner, D. M., & Wheatley, T. (1999). Apparent mental causation: Sources of the experience of will. *American Psychologist, 54*(7), 480–492.

Wilson, J. (2019). Between scientism and abstractionism in the metaphysics of emergence. In S. Gibb, R. Hendry, & T. Lancaster (Eds.), *The Routledge Handbook of Philosophy of Emergence*, 157–176. Routledge.

Winning, J., & Bechtel, W. (2019). Being emergence vs. pattern emergence: complexity, control, and goal-directedness in biological systems. In S. Gibb, R. Hendry, & T. Lancaster (Eds.), *The Routledge Handbook of Philosophy of Emergence*, 134–144. Routledge.

Wolraich, M. L., Chan, E., Froehlich, T., et al. (2019). ADHD diagnosis and treatment guidelines: A historical perspective. *Pediatrics, 144*(4). https://doi .org/10.1542/peds.2019-1682.

Woltering, S., Liu, Z., Rokeach, A., & Tannock, R. (2013). Neurophysiological differences in inhibitory control between adults with ADHD and their peers. *Neuropsychologia, 51*(10), 1888–1895.

Wu, W. (2011). What is conscious attention? *Philosophy and Phenomenological Research, 82*(1), 93–120.

Wu, W. (2014). *Attention*. New Problems of Philosophy Series. Routledge.

Wu, W. (2016). Experts and deviants: The story of agentive control. *Philosophy and Phenomenological Research, 93*(1), 101–126.

Yoshimi, J. (2012a). Supervenience, dynamical systems theory, and non-reductive physicalism. *British Journal for the Philosophy of Science, 63*(2), 373–398.

Yoshimi, J. (2012b). Active internalism and open dynamical systems. *Philosophical Psychology, 25*(1), 1–24.

Acknowledgments

Many thanks to Keith Frankish, Brian McLaughlin, Jeff Yoshimi, and the anonymous reviewers for helpful comments on earlier drafts of this manuscript.

Cambridge Elements $\equiv$

Philosophy of Mind

Keith Frankish

The University of Sheffield

Keith Frankish is a philosopher specializing in philosophy of mind, philosophy of psychology, and philosophy of cognitive science. He is the author of *Mind and Supermind* (Cambridge University Press, 2004) and *Consciousness* (2005), and has also edited or coedited several collections of essays, including *The Cambridge Handbook of Cognitive Science* (Cambridge University Press, 2012), *The Cambridge Handbook of Artificial Intelligence* (Cambridge University Press, 2014) (both with William Ramsey), and *Illusionism as a Theory of Consciousness* (2017).

About the Series

This series provides concise, authoritative introductions to contemporary work in philosophy of mind, written by leading researchers and including both established and emerging topics. It provides an entry point to the primary literature and will be the standard resource for researchers, students, and anyone wanting a firm grounding in this fascinating field.

Cambridge Elements $\equiv$

Philosophy of Mind